HOW TO ACT
&
THINK LIKE A CEO

Managing the Mindset of a Successful Leader

By

Cecil L. Dowdell

Copyright Page

Published by:

Cecil L. Dowdell Publishing

United States of America

Cover Design: Cecil L. Dowdell

Interior Formatting: ChatGPT-Assisted

ISBN: 979-8-2766-6788-1

Print Edition

Printed in the United States of America.

Dedication

This book is dedicated to everyone who has ever felt called to something greater…

to those who refused to settle, refused to shrink, and refused to let life define their limits.

To the leaders rising quietly,

to the dreamers who keep pushing,

to the ones who carry responsibility on their shoulders

and purpose in their hearts—

this is for you.

To my family, whose love, support, and belief in me gave me the strength to keep moving forward.

And to every person who has ever trusted my leadership,

you helped shape the vision behind these pages.

May this book remind you that greatness is not given—

it is built.

And may it inspire you to step boldly into the leader

you were always meant to become.

Acknowledgments

I want to express my deepest gratitude to everyone who supported, encouraged, and believed in me throughout this journey. Writing this book required discipline, patience, and purpose—and I am blessed to have people in my life who continue to remind me of my strength and potential.

To my family: thank you for your love, your guidance, and your unwavering support. Your belief in me gave me the courage to rise, lead, and keep moving forward even when the road wasn't easy.

To the mentors, leaders, and individuals who inspired my growth—you helped shape the wisdom and perspective on these pages. Your influence strengthened my mindset and helped me become the leader I am today.

To every reader holding this book: thank you.

Thank you for choosing growth.

Thank you for choosing leadership.

Thank you for choosing to elevate your life and mindset.

This book was written for you—

the rising leader, the hungry learner, the person determined to think and act like a CEO in every area of your life.

Your journey matters.

Your purpose matters.

And I am honored to be a part of your growth.

Table of Contents

CHAPTER 1 — The Decision to Lead Yourself

Leadership does not begin with a title, a team, or a business. It begins the moment you make the decision to take control of your own life. Before anyone follows you, you must learn to lead yourself with clarity, purpose, and discipline. Every CEO—no matter how successful—starts at this exact point: choosing responsibility over excuses, direction over confusion, and growth over comfort.

Leading yourself means accepting that your life is your business. Your habits, thoughts, relationships, health, energy, and daily decisions form the structure of that business. When you choose to step into leadership, you are declaring that you will no longer operate on autopilot. You are choosing intention. You are choosing to build, not drift.

This decision separates those who watch life happen from those who shape it. Many people want change, but few take ownership. They wait for the right moment, the perfect conditions, or someone to give them permission. CEOs don't wait—they move. They create momentum by taking responsibility for their direction and outcomes.

Leading yourself also means being brutally honest with your strengths and weaknesses. You cannot elevate until you evaluate. CEOs constantly assess where they are, where they want to go, and what must improve. This level of self-awareness becomes your blueprint for growth. Without it, you operate blindly, hoping success appears. With it, you create goals that align with who you want to become.

Your decision to lead yourself will also require sacrifice. Growth demands letting go of old patterns—whether that's procrastination, negative environments, inconsistent habits, or fear-driven thinking. Leadership requires you to rise above your comfort zone.

The life you want will always live on the other side of who you currently are. The transition begins the moment you decide to evolve, even when it feels uncomfortable.

Taking control of your life also builds internal respect. When you make promises to yourself and keep them, you develop confidence. When you set standards and enforce them, you build self-trust. When you stop making excuses, you strengthen your personal power. This internal foundation becomes the engine of every future success.

The decision to lead yourself also unlocks clarity. When you stop operating from emotion and start operating from intention, your path becomes more defined. You start seeing what truly matters… and what is wasting your time. You stop settling for distractions. You begin building instead of reacting. Clarity makes you dangerous—in the best way.

Every CEO knows this: discipline may be difficult, but regret is far harder. Growth may be uncomfortable, but being stuck is painful. Taking responsibility may be challenging, but being powerless is worse. Once you choose to lead yourself, you stop negotiating your future with excuses.

Your transformation begins with one powerful shift:

"My life is my responsibility, and I'm ready to lead it."

This one decision becomes the foundation for everything in your journey. It shapes how you think, how you move, and how you rise. When you commit to leading yourself first, you unlock the mindset required to lead others, build wealth, create impact, and reach levels you once doubted were possible.

The first chapter isn't about becoming a CEO of a company.

It's about becoming the CEO of *you.*

CHAPTER 2 — Thinking Like a Visionary

A CEO's power doesn't come from reacting to what is happening today—it comes from seeing what is possible tomorrow. Vision separates leaders from followers. It separates movement from stagnation. It separates those who build the future from those who merely live in it.

Thinking like a visionary requires you to expand your mental horizon. Most people think only about the next week or the next month. CEOs think in years. Visionaries think in decades. They see the long game even when they are still standing at the starting line.

Your vision is the picture of the life you want to create. It is not limited by your current challenges, income, environment, or past mistakes. It is shaped by your potential, not your circumstances. A visionary does not ask, "What can I have right now?" but instead asks, "What can I build if I stay focused and consistent?"

Vision requires imagination. It requires courage. More importantly, it requires the willingness to believe in something before it exists. Every major success in history—every company, invention, breakthrough, and transformation—began as a vision in someone's mind. CEOs understand that if you cannot see it internally, you will never achieve it externally.

To think like a visionary, you must train your mind to zoom out. Don't just look at what's in front of you—look at the entire landscape. Look at where you are, where you want to go, and what stands between the two. Look at your strengths, resources, and opportunities. Look at the people around you. Look at the habits that are either pushing you forward or holding you back.

Visionaries also think beyond themselves. They think about the people they will impact, the legacy they will create, and the value they will bring to the world. When your vision includes something larger than personal gain, it becomes stronger and more meaningful. Purpose always fuels consistency.

Another key part of visionary thinking is learning to anticipate. While most people only respond to problems, CEOs project them ahead of time. They ask questions such as:

- What will this decision look like in six months?
- What are the long-term consequences of this choice?
- What opportunities will exist that don't exist yet?
- How can I position myself right now to benefit later?

This ability to think ahead allows you to make strategic moves instead of emotional ones. It prevents impulsive decisions and helps you build with intention.

Visionaries also understand timing. They know when to move fast and when to wait. They know when to build and when to refine. They know that growth is a process, not an instant reward.

But the most important part of visionary thinking is belief. You must believe that you are capable of building a life far bigger than your current circumstances. You don't need permission. You don't need approval. You only need conviction.

Your vision becomes the blueprint for your life. It becomes the filter for your decisions, the fuel for your discipline, and the reason you keep going when the path gets hard. The clearer your vision, the more powerful your actions become.

Thinking like a visionary isn't about predicting the future. It's about creating it.

When you begin to think this way, you stop focusing on what is and start focusing on what can be. You stop playing small and start building something meaningful. You stop drifting and start directing.

A visionary mindset upgrades every part of your life. It strengthens your leadership, improves your decision-making, and sharpens your purpose. It transforms you from someone who reacts to life into someone who designs it.

Your vision is your compass.

Your vision is your roadmap.

Your vision is your future already speaking to you.

Once you commit to thinking like a visionary, the world opens up in ways you never imagined.

CHAPTER 3 — Discipline: The Foundation of All CEOs

Talent may open the first door, but discipline keeps every door open. Discipline is the unseen force behind every successful CEO. It is the habit of showing up when you don't feel like it, remaining focused when distractions appear, and doing the work even when comfort tries to pull you away from your purpose.

Many people dream big but live small because they lack discipline. They start projects but never finish. They commit to goals but abandon them at the first sign of discomfort. CEOs rise above this pattern because they understand one truth: **discipline creates freedom**. The more disciplined you are, the more control you have over your time, your goals, your income, and your future.

Discipline is not about perfection—it's about consistency. You don't need to be flawless. You only need to be committed. Progress compounds when you show up daily, even in small ways. Every workout, every chapter written, every hour of study, every business decision—over time these create unstoppable momentum.

The disciplined person becomes more powerful than the naturally talented person. Why? Because talent fades when not used, but discipline builds strength daily. When you train your mind to follow through, you become unstoppable.

One of the biggest lessons CEOs understand is that discipline is built, not born. No one is naturally disciplined. You develop it by making decisions that align with your goals instead of your feelings. Feelings want comfort. Discipline wants progress. CEOs choose progress.

Discipline starts with setting standards. You cannot rise without rules for yourself. These standards can be small at first—waking up on time, finishing what you start, keeping your promises, staying organized, or prioritizing what matters over what's easy. When you keep these standards consistently, you build self-respect. And when you respect yourself, discipline becomes a natural extension of who you are.

Another important part of discipline is eliminating excuses. Excuses are the enemy of growth. They sound reasonable, but they steal your potential. CEOs don't negotiate with excuses; they destroy them. They understand that you cannot build an extraordinary life using ordinary habits.

Discipline also protects your vision. When you know what you want, discipline becomes the guardrail that keeps you on the path. Without it, your goals become wishful thinking. With it, your goals become inevitable. Consistency makes results predictable.

One powerful truth about discipline is that it simplifies life. When you create structure, you remove chaos. When you have routines, you remove confusion. When you focus your energy, you remove overwhelm. CEOs love discipline because it gives them clarity and control.

It's also important to understand that discipline gets easier over time. At first, it feels like a challenge. Then it becomes a habit. Eventually, it becomes your identity. You no longer have to force yourself—you act automatically because discipline has become who you are.

Your environment plays a massive role in your discipline. Surround yourself with people who lift you, challenge you, and push you to grow—not those who encourage laziness, drama, or negativity. Your environment either strengthens your discipline or destroys it.

Finally, discipline requires patience. Real success doesn't happen overnight. You must be willing to stay committed long after the excitement wears off. CEOs become successful because they outlast everyone else. They stay the course when others quit.

Discipline is your superpower. It is the bridge between the life you have and the life you want. When you master discipline, you become dangerous—in the best possible way. You become someone impossible to stop, impossible to distract, and impossible to defeat.

If you want to think and perform like a CEO, start with discipline.

Everything else in your life will rise to meet it.

CHAPTER 4 — The Power of Personal Accountability

Accountability is one of the most powerful leadership principles on the planet. It is the ability to look at your life and say, "Everything I am and everything I am not is a result of my decisions." This level of truth is rare—but it is also the foundation of every great CEO.

Personal accountability means taking full ownership of your actions, your habits, your results, and your direction. It means refusing to blame people, circumstances, or the past for where you are. Blame may feel comfortable, but accountability creates power. CEOs choose power.

When you hold yourself accountable, you take control of your story. You step out of the role of a victim and into the role of a leader. Victims wait for solutions. Leaders create them. Victims wait for permission. Leaders give themselves permission. Accountability removes limits because it removes excuses.

People often misunderstand accountability. They think it means being hard on yourself or living in constant pressure, but accountability is actually a form of freedom. When you take ownership, you gain the ability to change anything in your life. What you own, you can fix. What you deny, you stay stuck in.

Accountability also builds trust—trust within yourself and trust from others. When people know you do what you say, finish what you start, and handle your responsibilities, they see you as reliable, consistent, and strong. This is why accountability is one of the first traits top leaders look for; they know it cannot be faked.

To practice personal accountability, you must begin with honesty. Not emotional honesty, but factual honesty. Look at your habits, your results, your productivity, your finances, your relationships, and your goals. Ask yourself:

- Am I truly giving my best?
- Am I doing the work I know I need to do?
- Am I avoiding responsibility by blaming people or situations?
- Am I operating at the level I expect from others?
- Am I taking ownership of my failures—not just my wins?

These questions are not meant to shame you but to strengthen you. Accountability is not a punishment; it is a mirror. And once you see clearly, you can make powerful decisions.

One of the biggest differences between average performers and CEOs is how they handle mistakes. Average people hide them. CEOs study them. Average people fear failure. CEOs analyze it, adjust, and move forward. Accountability allows you to use every experience as fuel instead of setbacks.

Another important aspect of accountability is discipline with your words. When you make a commitment—to yourself or others—you must honor it. Your word becomes your contract. CEOs understand that every broken promise weakens their internal power. Every kept promise strengthens it.

Personal accountability also means managing your emotions. You might not control everything that happens, but you control how you respond. Emotional control is part of ownership. Instead of reacting impulsively, CEOs respond strategically. They understand that emotional discipline protects their goals and maintains their credibility.

A key advantage of living with accountability is clarity. Once you stop making excuses, your next steps become obvious. You start seeing solutions instead of problems. You start taking action instead of hesitating. You start making progress instead of repeating old patterns.

Accountability is also contagious. When you lead yourself with high standards, people around you naturally rise. Your consistency inspires others. Your example shifts the environment. Accountability raises the temperature of the entire room.

Most importantly, accountability builds confidence. When you know you can rely on yourself, you move differently. You make decisions with strength. You act with certainty. You trust your judgment. This self-trust becomes an invisible force that guides every future success.

The truth is simple:

If you want a better life, hold yourself to a better standard.

If you want greater success, take greater ownership.

If you want to think like a CEO, embrace accountability daily.

The moment you stop blaming and start owning is the moment your life begins to transform.

CHAPTER 5 — Developing CEO-Level Confidence

Confidence is not a personality trait—it's a skill. It's something you build, strengthen, and reinforce through deliberate daily actions. CEOs are not confident because they are in positions of power; they are in positions of power because they developed confidence long before anyone recognized their leadership.

CEO-level confidence is grounded, steady, and unshakeable. It doesn't rely on external validation, compliments, or applause. It comes from internal certainty—certainty in your abilities, your discipline, your standards, and your willingness to grow. True confidence forms when you trust yourself more than you fear challenges.

To build this type of confidence, you must first understand where confidence truly comes from: **repetition, results, and resilience.**

1. Repetition: Doing the Work Until You Become Strong

Confidence grows when you repeatedly show up. Every time you practice a skill, follow a routine, or keep a promise to yourself, you strengthen your belief in your capabilities. CEOs aren't confident because they know everything—they're confident because they consistently put in the work to improve.

Repetition builds competence. Competence builds confidence.

When you do something enough times, fear disappears and mastery emerges.

2. Results: Earning Proof Through Action

Confidence is built when you see progress, no matter how small. Every win—every finished task, every healthy decision, every problem solved—adds a brick to your internal foundation. CEOs pay attention to these wins. They collect evidence that they are becoming stronger, smarter, and more capable.

Instead of focusing on what they can't do yet, they focus on what they are actively improving.

This shift transforms self-doubt into forward motion.

3. Resilience: Getting Back Up Stronger

Confidence isn't built by avoiding failure—it's built by surviving it. Every challenge you overcome becomes a reminder that you can handle more than you thought. CEOs understand that failure is not a threat to confidence; it is the fuel that strengthens it.

When you handle setbacks with resilience, you build a version of yourself that is unbreakable.

Developing CEO-level confidence also requires separating your identity from your insecurities. Many people walk through life tied to past experiences, mistakes, criticism, or environments that never believed in them. CEOs break those mental chains. They rewrite their identity through intentional action, not emotional memories.

To build this level of confidence, you must speak to yourself differently. Your internal dialogue matters. When you feed your mind fear, doubt, or negativity, you weaken your potential. But when you feed it strength, certainty, and direction, you elevate your entire performance.

Confidence is also tied to preparation. When you prepare for your goals—learning, studying, improving your mindset, practicing your skills—you naturally feel more capable. Preparation removes fear because fear lives in the unknown. CEOs prepare relentlessly, so they step into situations with clarity and certainty.

Another key element is posture and presence. Confidence is not arrogance; it is alignment. It is the ability to stand tall, move intentionally, speak with clarity, and maintain control of your energy. When you carry yourself with structure, the world treats you differently. Your presence becomes a statement.

Confidence also grows when you honor your standards. Every time you maintain discipline—even in private—you reinforce your identity as someone who follows through. Consistency builds credibility, and credibility builds confidence. You can't fake confidence when your habits don't match your goals.

And most importantly, confidence requires courage.

You cannot become confident by staying comfortable.

You cannot grow by avoiding challenges.

You cannot strengthen your belief by shrinking your goals.

Courage means taking the first step even when you're unsure.

Confidence is created by taking the next step until you no longer doubt.

CEO-level confidence is not loud, flashy, or arrogant. It is calm, grounded, and powerful. It is the quiet understanding that you can handle whatever comes your way. It is the feeling of being prepared, aligned, and focused. It is the belief that you are capable of continually evolving into someone greater.

Once you develop this level of confidence, you will think differently, move differently, speak differently, and lead differently. It becomes part of your identity—and once confidence becomes who you are, success becomes a natural outcome.

CHAPTER 6 — Eliminating Average Thinking

Average thinking is the silent killer of potential. It keeps people stuck, comfortable, unmotivated, and unaware of what they are truly capable of. CEOs rise above the average mindset because they understand that extraordinary results require extraordinary thinking. You cannot live an exceptional life with a mediocre mindset.

Eliminating average thinking begins with awareness. Most people don't realize they're thinking small because average has become normal. They limit themselves without questioning why. They settle for less because they've been conditioned to believe that "less" is all they deserve. CEOs break that conditioning by challenging every belief that holds them back.

Average thinking is rooted in fear — fear of failure, fear of judgment, fear of discomfort, fear of standing out. People hide behind excuses because stepping into greatness feels risky. But CEOs understand a powerful truth: **comfort is far more dangerous than risk**. Comfort keeps you stagnant. Risk moves you forward.

To eliminate average thinking, you must learn to think in possibilities instead of limitations. Average minds see obstacles; CEO minds see opportunities. Average minds see problems; CEO minds see strategies. Average minds see fear; CEO minds see growth. The difference is not intelligence — it's perspective.

Another characteristic of average thinking is emotional decision-making. People let their feelings dictate their actions. If they feel tired, they stop. If they feel unsure, they quit. If they feel uncomfortable, they avoid. CEOs break free from emotional control by learning to act based on standards, not moods. They understand that feelings are temporary, but standards build legacies.

Average thinking also shows up in how people talk. Words shape beliefs, and beliefs shape behavior. When someone says, "It's too hard," "I can't do that," or "Maybe one day," they shrink their own potential. CEOs use language that empowers their mindset: "I will figure it out," "I will grow into it," "I will find a way." Words become weapons when used correctly.

Another key part of eliminating average thinking is upgrading your environment. People absorb the energy around them. If you surround yourself with complainers, doubters, or people who settle, your mind automatically sinks toward their level. CEOs place themselves around ambition, excellence, and discipline. They understand that environment is not just a place — it is a mentality.

Eliminating average thinking also requires breaking the habit of instant gratification. Average thinkers want results now. CEOs want results that last. When you value comfort over progress, you stay average. But when you embrace delayed gratification — working now for a better future — your entire life shifts.

One of the strongest signs of average thinking is a lack of goals. People wander through life without direction because they've never asked themselves what they truly want. CEOs do the opposite. They think deeply, plan intentionally, and set goals that stretch their identity. They don't aim for what's easy; they aim for what's meaningful.

To rise above average thinking, you must question everything:

- Why do I believe what I believe?
- Are my habits aligned with my goals?
- Have I been settling without realizing it?
- Am I making decisions based on fear or vision?
- Am I living to impress others or to fulfill my potential?

These questions create breakthroughs. They force you to confront the difference between the life you have and the life you want.

Eliminating average thinking also means removing excuses. Excuses are mental shortcuts that justify staying small. CEOs take responsibility instead. They know that growth demands effort, discomfort, and resilience. They embrace those challenges because they understand they lead to transformation.

The final step in eliminating average thinking is adopting a high-performance mindset. This means pursuing excellence in everything you do — not perfection, but excellence. It means showing up fully, even when no one is watching. It means refusing to half-commit, half-try, or half-believe.

Average thinking is easy. Excellence is earned.

But the reward for eliminating average thinking is freedom —

freedom to grow, freedom to lead, and freedom to build a life worthy of your potential.

Once you break away from average, you never want to return.

Your mind becomes sharper, your decisions become bolder, and your path becomes clearer.

You stop thinking like everyone else…

and you start thinking like a CEO

CHAPTER 7 — Building an Unshakable Work Ethic

A strong work ethic is the force that separates dreamers from doers. It is the internal engine that drives execution, consistency, and long-term success. CEOs are not defined by their titles—they are defined by their ability to outwork, outthink, and outlast everyone around them. An unshakable work ethic isn't about working nonstop; it's about working with intention, discipline, and purpose.

A powerful work ethic begins with your standards. You cannot perform at a high level with low expectations for yourself. CEOs set standards that demand excellence: showing up early, being prepared, taking responsibility, and executing tasks with precision. When your standards rise, everything about your work rises with them.

But a strong work ethic is not about grinding blindly. It is about consistency. Anyone can work hard for a day. Few can do it for years. CEOs win because they show up with the same energy on the days they feel motivated and the days they don't. They understand that consistency compounds—and over time, it becomes unstoppable momentum.

Your work ethic also reflects your character. It shows your commitment, your resilience, your discipline, and your integrity. When you work hard even when no one is watching, you build internal strength that people can feel. Work ethic is a silent language; it communicates who you are far more loudly than words.

To build an unshakable work ethic, you must train your mind to do hard things without hesitation. Most people avoid difficulty. CEOs embrace it. Hard work sharpens your skills, strengthens your identity, and separates you from average performers. When you learn to lean into challenges instead of avoiding them, you become mentally unbreakable.

A strong work ethic also requires structure. High performers don't just hope to get things done—they plan it. They schedule their priorities, protect their time, and operate with intention. They build routines that support their goals, not distract from them. Structure isn't restrictive—it's empowering. It ensures that your effort produces results, not chaos.

Another key part of work ethic is your relationship with excuses. People with average mindsets let excuses control their outcomes: "I'm tired," "It's too hard," "I'll do it later." CEOs remove excuses from their vocabulary. They understand that excuses are the quickest way to destroy momentum. When you eliminate excuses, productivity becomes your natural state.

Your environment also influences your work ethic. If you're surrounded by people who complain, procrastinate, make excuses, or settle for mediocrity, you will naturally absorb their energy. CEOs place themselves around disciplined, driven individuals who expect excellence. Iron sharpens iron.

Building an unshakable work ethic also means learning to work smart. CEOs don't try to do everything—they focus on the highest-impact tasks. They prioritize progress over busywork. They delegate, automate, and simplify. They aim for results, not effort for the sake of effort. Smart work multiplies the power of hard work.

Another essential factor in work ethic is emotional discipline. You cannot build a strong work ethic if you allow your emotions to dictate your productivity. Some days you'll feel motivated; other days you won't. You must work regardless. CEOs train themselves to act based on purpose, not mood. When purpose becomes the driver, your work ethic becomes untouchable.

A powerful work ethic also requires recovery. You must take care of your mind, body, and energy. CEOs know that burnout comes from lack of balance, not too much ambition. They rest intentionally, recharge strategically, and protect their mental clarity. A rested mind works better than an exhausted one. High-level work ethic includes sustainability.

The final piece of building an unshakable work ethic is accountability. Hold yourself to your commitments. Track your progress. Review your results. Celebrate wins and study losses. When you take ownership of your performance, your work ethic becomes a living force—strong, consistent, and unstoppable.

Work ethic is not something you are born with.

It is something you build.

It is something you reinforce.

It is something you choose every single day.

When you commit to developing an unshakable work ethic, you separate yourself from 99% of people instantly. You become the person who doesn't quit, who doesn't make excuses, who doesn't break under pressure. You become the one who shows up, delivers, and executes.

This is how CEOs operate.

This is how leaders are built.

This is how powerful lives are created.

CHAPTER 8 — Mental Toughness in High-Pressure Moments

Pressure doesn't create weakness — it reveals it. And it doesn't create strength — it exposes it. CEOs operate in environments where pressure is constant: deadlines, decisions, risks, responsibility, expectations, and scrutiny. What separates a high-level leader from everyone else is their ability to remain calm, focused, and effective when the stakes are highest.

Mental toughness is not about being emotionless or pretending challenges don't affect you. It's about staying in control of your thoughts, your reactions, and your decisions when life demands your best. It's the internal strength that allows you to stay steady in chaos, resilient under stress, and unshaken by obstacles.

To build mental toughness, you must first accept a truth: pressure is unavoidable. You cannot escape it, but you can prepare for it. CEOs don't wish for less pressure — they develop the mindset and skills to handle more.

1. Control Your Reaction, Not the Situation

The first step in mental toughness is emotional discipline. You cannot control every problem, every challenge, or every unexpected twist in life — but you can control your response. Most people react impulsively. They panic. They freeze. They get angry. They quit. This emotional reaction makes the situation worse.

CEOs train themselves to pause, breathe, observe, and respond with clarity.

They ask:

- What is the problem?
- What is within my control?
- What is the next best move?

This calm decision-making becomes their advantage.

2. Build Pressure Tolerance Through Exposure

You don't become mentally tough by avoiding discomfort. You build toughness by facing it. Every difficult task, intense situation, or challenging environment is a training ground. The more you expose yourself to controlled pressure — deadlines, goals, hard conversations, new responsibilities — the stronger you become.

This is why CEOs grow so quickly: they consistently operate outside their comfort zone.

3. Stay Goal-Focused, Not Emotion-Focused

In high-pressure moments, emotions try to take the wheel. Fear, doubt, frustration, and uncertainty can cloud judgment. Mentally tough individuals shift their attention back to the mission. They think in solutions, not emotions. They ask themselves:

- What matters most right now?
- What action moves me forward?
- What outcome am I committed to?

This shift in focus allows them to act with precision instead of panic.

4. Keep Your Composure Under Fire

Composure is a superpower. People follow leaders who stay calm under pressure. If you break, the environment breaks. If you stay structured, others mirror your strength. Mental toughness means maintaining your presence, tone, and clarity even when you feel the weight of the situation.

A calm mind makes better decisions than a chaotic one.

5. Turn Obstacles Into an Advantage

Pressure reveals opportunities. Where others see stress, CEOs see strategy. Challenges force creativity. Problems spark innovation. Obstacles create leaders. Mentally tough people don't run from tough moments — they use them as leverage to rise.

Every struggle is a step toward expansion.

6. Practice Self-Control Daily

Mental toughness isn't built overnight. It's built through daily habits:

- Keeping your promises
- Finishing what you start
- Pushing through discomfort
- Staying disciplined
- Managing your energy
- Controlling your impulses

Each act of self-control strengthens your mental resilience.

7. Protect Your Mind From Negativity

Your mental environment matters. Doubts, fear-driven people, negativity, drama, and gossip weaken resilience. CEOs protect their minds fiercely. They surround themselves with strong thinkers, solution-driven individuals, and people who elevate, not drain, their mental strength.

A tough mind requires a healthy environment.

8. Trust Your Training

Confidence is essential during pressure. You must trust the work you've done, the skills you've built, and the challenges you've overcome. When high-pressure moments hit, your preparation becomes your anchor.

Mental toughness is not the absence of fear —

it is the mastery of fear.

It is the ability to keep moving when others freeze.

It is the discipline to remain steady when others panic.

It is the strength to continue despite uncertainty.

When you build mental toughness, pressure becomes fuel.

Stress becomes strategy.

Challenges become teachers.

Obstacles become stepping stones.

With mental toughness, you become the calm in the storm, the leader people trust, and the force no setback can break.

CHAPTER 9 — Turning Problems Into Opportunities

One of the greatest differences between average thinkers and CEOs is how they view problems. Most people see problems as interruptions, setbacks, or reasons to quit. CEOs see problems as information, opportunities, and moments to innovate. This mindset shift is one of the most powerful skills a leader can develop.

A problem is not a dead end — it's a doorway. It forces you to think differently, act smarter, and grow stronger. Problems show you where improvement is needed. They reveal weaknesses in your system. They push you to elevate your thinking. CEOs welcome this process, because they know that every problem carries the seed of a solution that can move them forward.

Turning problems into opportunities begins with perspective.

When something goes wrong, the average person asks, "Why is this happening to me?"

The CEO asks, "What is this trying to teach me?"

One question creates frustration.

The other creates clarity.

1. Problems Reveal Possibility

Every major breakthrough in business, leadership, or personal development has come from identifying and solving a problem. When something doesn't work, it opens the door for something better to be created. CEOs don't fear problems — they study them. They understand that problems signal opportunity.

A problem might reveal:

- A new system that needs to be built
- A better strategy than the current one
- A gap in knowledge or skill that must be improved
- A mindset that needs to be strengthened
- A product, service, or solution the world needs

When you start looking at problems through this lens, they become valuable assets.

2. Problems Make You Creative

Comfort kills creativity. Pressure activates it. When everything is easy, your mind becomes lazy. When things go wrong, your brain is forced to think deeper, innovate faster, and operate at a higher level.

CEOs thrive under this pressure because they understand that creativity is born in challenge.

Solutions only exist because problems exist.

3. Problems Build Leadership

Leadership is not tested when things are smooth — it's tested when things get difficult. A leader's true strength is revealed in how they respond to disruption, conflict, or unexpected challenges. Do they panic? Do they freeze? Or do they rise?

Turning problems into opportunities is how CEOs earn respect, trust, and influence.

People follow leaders who remain strategic while others fall apart.

4. Problems Strengthen You

Every problem you overcome makes you smarter, stronger, and more prepared for future challenges. CEOs build confidence by solving problems. They become more resilient, more adaptable, and more capable with each situation they conquer.

Each problem you solve becomes part of your leadership foundation.

5. Problems Provide Advantage

Most people avoid problems, complain about problems, or collapse under problems. This gives CEOs a massive advantage. While others retreat, leaders move forward. While others fear complexity, CEOs search for opportunity.

If you can remain calm, think clearly, and solve problems consistently, you rise above 90% of people instantly.

6. Problems Teach You to Think Strategically

CEOs use a structured approach when facing a problem. Instead of reacting emotionally, they break the problem down:

- **What exactly is happening?**
- **What caused it?**
- **What can I control right now?**
- **What is the best immediate move?**
- **What is the long-term solution?**
- **How can this make me or my business stronger?**

This strategic breakdown turns confusion into clarity and chaos into action.

7. Problems Force Growth

Growth never comes from staying comfortable. Problems force you to stretch your skills, upgrade your mindset, and operate at a higher level. CEOs grow rapidly because they face problems daily — and they learn from every one of them.

Growth is uncomfortable, but it is always worth it.

8. Problems Are Opportunities in Disguise

Some opportunities are clear — others are hidden. The hidden ones are almost always disguised as problems. When you learn to look beyond the surface, you begin to spot openings that others miss.

- A problem at work may lead to a promotion.
- A financial setback may spark smarter money habits.
- A failed attempt may reveal a better method.
- A mistake may teach you something that prevents a bigger failure later.

Every problem has a purpose if you choose to see it.

The difference between frustration and opportunity is perspective.

The difference between quitting and growing is mindset.

The difference between average and CEO-level thinking is how you respond when things go wrong.

When you learn to turn problems into opportunities, you stop fearing challenges and start using them as fuel. You become more strategic, more resilient, and more powerful. You stop running from difficulty — and you start rising through it.

This is how leaders are built.

This is how winners think.

This is how CEOs operate.

CHAPTER 10 — Becoming a Strategic Thinker

Strategic thinking is the skill that elevates you from reacting to life… to directing it. It is the ability to look beyond the surface, analyze the bigger picture, anticipate outcomes, and make decisions that move you toward long-term success. CEOs excel because they don't think like everyone else—they think **strategically**, deliberately, and with intention.

Most people focus only on what is directly in front of them. They think in days or weeks. CEOs think in months, years, and decades. They operate with a wide-angle lens, making decisions not just for today, but for the future they want to create.

To become a strategic thinker, you must shift from short-term survival to long-term success.

1. Think Beyond the Immediate Moment

Strategic thinkers ask themselves:

- "What does this decision look like 6 months from now?"
- "What are the long-term consequences?"
- "How does this fit into my bigger vision?"

Average thinkers focus on comfort.

Strategic thinkers focus on outcomes.

2. Anticipate Instead of Reacting

Most people respond only when problems arrive. CEOs anticipate problems before they appear. They scan the environment, identify risks, and prepare solutions in advance. This proactive mindset reduces stress, improves performance, and protects the mission.

Strategic thinkers stay ahead because they see what others don't.

3. Analyze Patterns and Make Intelligent Adjustments

Strategic thinking requires the ability to identify patterns:

- What's working?
- What's slowing you down?
- What needs to be improved?
- What should be eliminated completely?

When you study your patterns, you gain insight into your behavior, productivity, strengths, and weaknesses. CEOs constantly refine their strategy based on this information. They improve quickly because they evaluate consistently.

4. Understand the Difference Between Urgent and Important

Many people stay busy but never move forward. They get trapped in urgency—responding to everything as if it's a crisis. CEOs prioritize what is important, not just what is loud. Strategic thinkers protect their time, energy, and focus by filtering their priorities through purpose.

What aligns with your long-term mission matters more than what demands your attention in the moment.

5. Think in Systems, Not Scattered Actions

Strategic thinkers build systems—repeatable processes that produce consistent results. Instead of tackling every task as a new challenge, they create structure. They automate what they can, delegate what they should, and focus on what only they can do.

Systems create efficiency.

Efficiency creates freedom.

Freedom creates growth.

6. Let Logic Lead, Not Emotion

Emotional decisions are short-sighted. Strategic decisions are long-term. CEOs control their emotions to protect their judgment. They pause, assess, calculate, and choose with intention. They think before moving because they understand that one careless decision can cost time, energy, money, or opportunity.

Strategic thinkers stay steady—never impulsive.

7. Ask High-Level Questions

The quality of your thinking depends on the quality of your questions. Strategic thinkers constantly ask questions such as:

- "What's the real goal here?"
- "What options haven't I considered yet?"
- "What resources can help me move faster?"
- "What outcome am I truly trying to achieve?"
- "What is the smartest—not the easiest—move?"

These questions sharpen your decisions and open doors average thinkers never see.

8. See Opportunity in Every Scenario

Strategic thinkers understand that every situation—good or bad—can be leveraged. They find advantage in setbacks, openings in problems, and lessons in failure. This mindset makes them adaptable, resilient, and unstoppable in uncertain environments.

Where others see obstacles, CEOs see strategy.

9. Think Long-Term While Executing Daily

Strategic thinking requires balance:

Vision for the future + Execution in the present.

You plan long-term, but act daily.

You dream big, but move consistently.

You see the bigger picture, but handle today with precision.

This blend of vision and action creates unstoppable progress.

10. Always Play Three Moves Ahead

The best CEOs don't think about the next step—they think about the step after that, and the step after that. They predict outcomes, prepare contingencies, and make moves that position them for future success.

This forward-thinking approach makes them nearly impossible to catch off guard.

Strategic thinking is a discipline.

A skill.

A mindset.

And a competitive advantage.

When you master it, you become more efficient, more effective, more confident, and far more powerful in every area of your life.

You stop reacting…

and you start directing.

You stop drifting…

and you start leading.

You stop thinking like everyone else…

and you begin thinking like a CEO.

CHAPTER 11 — Habit Systems of High-Level Leaders

Great leaders are not defined by their goals—they are defined by their habits. Goals give direction, but habits create transformation. CEOs understand that success isn't built in a single moment of inspiration; it's built through consistent, disciplined actions repeated every day until excellence becomes automatic.

High-level leaders don't rely on motivation. They rely on systems. A system is a structure—a repeatable process that guarantees progress, removes guesswork, and keeps you moving even when your mood changes. Systems turn ambition into results.

Most people try to change their lives through willpower alone. They set big goals, feel pumped for a few days, then lose momentum. CEOs avoid this cycle by designing habit systems that support their future identity. They don't hope for discipline—they build it into their lifestyle.

1. Start With Identity, Not Intensity

High-level leaders don't ask, "What do I want to achieve?" They ask, "Who do I want to become?"

This shift changes everything.

When you think in identity, your habits form naturally:

- A healthy person eats with intention.
- A disciplined person wakes up on time.
- A successful leader plans their day.
- A CEO-level thinker eliminates distractions.

Identity shapes behavior. When you decide who you are, consistent action becomes effortless.

2. Build Routines That Eliminate Uncertainty

Uncertainty kills performance. When you wake up without a plan, the world decides your day for you. CEOs take control of their morning, afternoon, and evening through structured routines. Not rigid schedules—**systems**.

A high-level morning routine may include:

- A moment of clarity (prayer, reflection, or stillness)
- Reviewing goals or priorities
- Physical movement
- Setting the top 3 tasks of the day

Evening routines may include:

- Reviewing progress
- Preparing the next day
- Resetting the environment
- Mental decompression to maintain clarity

Routines provide stability in a chaotic world.

3. Create a System for Focus

Leaders do not chase everything. They prioritize.

To maintain focus, CEOs use systems such as:

- Time-blocking
- Deep work sessions
- Removing notifications
- Avoiding pointless multitasking
- Protecting energy during productive hours

They understand that focus is a superpower in a distracted society.

4. Use Micro-Habits to Build Massive Progress

Change doesn't require dramatic action—it requires consistent action.

Micro-habits are small steps repeated daily, such as:

- Reading 10 minutes a day
- Cleaning your workspace for 2 minutes
- Writing one paragraph per day
- Exercising for 10 minutes
- Planning the next day each night

These small habits compound into massive transformation.

5. Automate What You Can

High-level leaders remove decision fatigue by automating routine choices.

Examples:

- Preparing meals in advance
- Using calendar reminders
- Scheduling financial transfers
- Automating bill payments
- Setting fixed times for planning or workouts

Automation frees your mind to focus on what truly matters.

6. Design an Environment That Supports Growth

Your environment shapes your habits more than willpower does. CEOs engineer their surroundings so success becomes the default. They remove distractions, eliminate clutter, and make productive choices convenient.

If your environment is aligned with your goals, your habits follow naturally.

7. Track Progress Consistently

What gets measured improves.

Leaders track their habits through:

- Journals
- Digital apps
- Weekly reviews
- Accountability partners

Tracking creates awareness. Awareness drives improvement.

8. Replace Bad Habits Instead of Forcing Them Away

The best way to eliminate a negative habit is to replace it with a better one.

Instead of:

- scrolling → read
- procrastinating → plan

- complaining → problem-solve
- reacting → reflecting

Replacement is far more effective than resistance.

9. Stay Flexible But Never Inconsistent

A system should guide you, not trap you. CEOs adjust when necessary—but they never abandon the mission. They adapt without losing momentum. Flexibility keeps you human. Consistency keeps you powerful.

10. Make Excellence the Default

High-level leaders operate with intentional standards. They don't do "just enough." They don't cut corners. They don't settle for average results. Their systems enforce excellence—even when no one is watching.

Habit systems are the silent architecture of greatness.

They turn discipline into a lifestyle, routine into identity, and small steps into extraordinary results.

When you build the right systems, success stops being unpredictable. It becomes inevitable.

CHAPTER 12 — Emotional Intelligence in Daily Leadership

Emotional intelligence (EQ) is one of the most important leadership skills in the world. You can be talented, disciplined, knowledgeable, and ambitious—but if you cannot manage your emotions or understand the emotions of others, your leadership will always have limits. CEOs rise to the top not just because they think well, but because they *feel* well. They know how to stay calm, communicate clearly, handle pressure, and connect with people in meaningful ways.

Emotional intelligence is not about being soft or overly emotional. It's about control. It's about understanding yourself so deeply that nothing and no one can pull you out of your power. It's about reading situations, navigating conflict, influencing people, and staying level-headed when the world around you feels chaotic.

There are four core pillars of emotional intelligence that every high-level leader must master: **self-awareness, self-management, social awareness, and relationship management.**

---

1. Self-Awareness: Mastering Your Internal World

Self-awareness is knowing what you feel and why you feel it. Most people move through life on emotional autopilot—reacting to situations without understanding their triggers. CEOs do not operate this way. They study themselves. They know their strengths, weaknesses, values, pressure points, and emotional tendencies.

Self-awareness allows you to:

- Recognize emotional triggers
- Catch yourself before reacting poorly
- Make clear decisions under pressure
- Understand how your mood affects your performance

- Stay aligned with your values and goals

You cannot lead others if you cannot lead your own emotions.

---

2. Self-Management: Controlling Your Reactions

Self-management is the ability to stay calm, stable, and disciplined regardless of circumstances. This is a superpower. Most people let emotions dictate their actions—anger, fear, impatience, frustration. CEOs manage their emotions with precision.

Self-management includes:

- Staying composed under stress
- Delaying emotional reactions
- Thinking before responding
- Redirecting negative energy into productive action
- Practicing patience and emotional discipline

The one who remains calm controls the situation.

---

3. Social Awareness: Reading People and Environments

Social awareness is the ability to sense emotions in others, understand group dynamics, and read the room. Leaders must be able to pick up on unspoken tension, hidden concerns, and emotional cues. Social awareness helps CEOs communicate effectively, make informed decisions, and build trust.

With strong social awareness, you can:

- Identify when someone is overwhelmed
- Sense shifts in energy or morale
- Understand how your message is received
- Adjust your communication style based on who you're speaking to
- Predict reactions before they happen

This is why emotionally intelligent leaders rarely misread situations—they see what others overlook.

---

4. Relationship Management: Influencing and Connecting With Others

Relationship management is the ability to build strong connections, communicate effectively, inspire people, and handle conflict gracefully. Leadership is not about authority—it's about influence. Influence requires emotional intelligence.

Relationship management includes:

- Having difficult conversations respectfully
- Motivating others with clarity and confidence
- Building trust through consistency
- Managing disagreements without damaging relationships
- Guiding people toward shared goals

People follow leaders who make them feel understood, valued, and respected.

Developing Emotional Intelligence

Emotional intelligence is not fixed—it can be built through conscious practice. Here are habits CEOs use daily:

• **Pause before reacting.**

A few seconds of reflection prevents hours of regret.

• **Ask questions instead of assuming.**

Curiosity replaces conflict.

• **Practice active listening.**

Listen to understand, not to respond.

• **Monitor your emotional triggers.**

When you know your patterns, you control them.

• **Keep your tone calm and controlled.**

Tone influences trust.

• **Approach problems with empathy, not ego.**

Understanding others creates cooperation.

• **Separate facts from emotions.**

Feelings are temporary—facts are stable.

• **Regulate stress through structure and routine.**

The more stability you create, the clearer you think.

• **Reflect at the end of each day.**

Review your emotional wins and emotional weaknesses.

These habits sharpen your emotional intelligence over time.

The Power of EQ in Leadership

Leaders with high emotional intelligence:

- Build stronger teams
- Make better decisions
- Handle pressure calmly
- Earn trust quickly
- Resolve conflict faster
- Communicate with clarity
- Inspire others naturally
- Navigate challenges with maturity

People follow leaders who make them feel safe, confident, and understood.

Emotional intelligence is how you build that kind of leadership presence.

When you master EQ, you become unshakeable.

You control the environment instead of being controlled by it.

You bring logic, stability, and clarity to every situation.

You show up as a leader people respect and rely on.

This is what separates average performers from elite-level CEOs.

CHAPTER 13 — The CEO Standard: Precision & Consistency

Success isn't built on big moments—it's built on the small decisions you make every day. What separates CEOs from average performers is their unwavering commitment to **precision** and **consistency**. These two qualities turn intention into execution and potential into results.

Precision is the ability to perform with accuracy, clarity, and purpose.

Consistency is the ability to perform with discipline, stability, and reliability.

Together, they form the CEO standard—a level of excellence that becomes non-negotiable.

Most people operate emotionally. They do things when they feel like it, and they do them however it happens. But CEOs operate with intention. They work with precision, show up consistently, and execute with excellence—even on the days they don't feel motivated.

---

1. Precision: Doing Things the Right Way

Precision is a mindset. It's the decision to do things properly, not sloppily. CEOs understand that the details matter because details determine quality.

Precision means:

- Speaking clearly instead of vaguely
- Planning with clarity instead of guessing
- Executing tasks fully, not halfway
- Preparing before acting
- Reviewing work for accuracy
- Paying attention to what others overlook

Precision builds credibility. When people see you operate with accuracy, they trust you more, respect you more, and rely on you more.

A person who moves with precision becomes known for excellence—even in small things.

---

2. Consistency: Showing Up the Same Way, Every Day

Consistency is the force that compounds progress. It is not about intensity—it's about reliability. Anyone can work hard for a few days, but successful leaders show up repeatedly, even when the excitement is gone.

Consistency means:

- Showing up on time
- Meeting deadlines
- Keeping your word
- Sticking to routines
- Following your plan
- Performing with effort every time

Consistency builds momentum.

Momentum builds confidence.

Confidence builds results.

When you show up consistently, success becomes predictable—not accidental.

---

3. The CEO Standard: No Excuses, No Half-Doing

People with average mindsets cut corners. They rush. They make excuses. They avoid accountability. CEOs reject this approach entirely. Excellence is their default setting.

The CEO standard means:

- If you start something, you finish it
- If you commit to it, you do it well
- If it has your name on it, it reflects your reputation
- If it matters, it deserves your best
- If you fail, you learn and improve

Nothing about this standard is based on perfection—it is based on responsibility.

When you take pride in how you operate, every result elevates automatically.

---

4. Precision Creates Power

Precision creates a level of clarity that eliminates confusion. When your actions are deliberate, you waste less time, energy, and effort. Precision also makes you more efficient because you stop guessing and start executing with purpose.

A precise thinker makes powerful decisions.

A precise worker delivers exceptional results.

A precise leader earns unwavering trust.

---

5. Consistency Creates Trust

People follow consistency, not inconsistency.

They follow the leader who:

- Shows up the same way every day
- Maintains emotional stability
- Follows through on responsibilities
- Delivers results repeatedly
- Sets a standard they can rely on

The more consistent you are, the more influence you gain.

Consistency is not flashy—but it is unstoppable.

---

6. Excellence Is a Habit, Not a Talent

Excellence is not something you do once.

It is something you do repeatedly.

To build the CEO standard, you must:

- Develop strong routines

- Create structure
- Prioritize what matters
- Eliminate unnecessary distractions
- Raise your personal expectations

Excellence becomes easy when it becomes a habit.

---

7. Precision + Consistency = Mastery

Mastery is built when you combine accuracy with repetition. A skill practiced correctly becomes powerful. A habit repeated with intention becomes a superpower.

Every high-level CEO follows this formula:

- Learn the skill
- Practice with precision
- Repeat with consistency
- Improve after every iteration

Most people never reach mastery because they lack one of the two ingredients:

They either work hard without strategy (lack precision)…

or have strategy without discipline (lack consistency).

CEOs master both.

---

8. The CEO Standard Elevates Every Area of Life

When you raise your standard of precision and consistency, everything improves:

- Your relationships
- Your health
- Your finances
- Your work
- Your personal goals
- Your leadership presence
- Your influence

People can feel the difference.

Your results begin to speak for you.

Your character becomes undeniable.

Precision is how you do it.

Consistency is how often you do it.

Excellence is what you become when the two align.

The CEO standard is not something you perform—it's something you live.

And once you operate at this level, you will never allow yourself to go back.

CHAPTER 14 — Leading Yourself When No One Is Watching

Real leadership begins in private. It's not built on titles, praise, or public recognition—it's built in the quiet moments when no one sees you, no one is cheering, and no one is checking your progress. CEOs rise to the top because they lead themselves with discipline and integrity long before the world ever acknowledges them.

Most people only put in effort when someone is watching. Their performance depends on external pressure or validation. But self-leadership is different. It demands that you show up for yourself, keep your promises, and maintain your standards even when there is no audience.

The greatest indicator of your future success is how you operate behind closed doors.

---

1. Private Discipline Builds Public Power

Your habits in private shape your results in public.

Do you prepare?

Do you study?

Do you practice?

Do you follow through?

Do you stay true to your goals?

The world only sees the outcome, but your private discipline creates the outcome. CEOs don't wait for applause—they perform because excellence is who they are, not something they pretend to be.

When no one is watching, your character takes the lead.

---

2. Integrity Means Doing the Right Thing—Even Alone

Integrity is not tested in front of others; it is tested when you're by yourself.

It's easy to be disciplined when someone expects it from you.

It's hard to stay disciplined when the only person holding you accountable is you.

But this is where true leadership is formed.

When you keep promises to yourself—wake up early, stay consistent, improve your skills, prepare your mind—you build internal confidence. You begin to trust yourself. And self-trust is the foundation of unstoppable leadership.

---

3. Your Private Standards Determine Your Public Success

High-level leaders have non-negotiable standards that they follow whether or not anyone sees it. They understand:

- If you cheat in private, you will fail in public.
- If you cut corners in private, you weaken your foundation.
- If you avoid difficult tasks in private, you crumble under pressure.

Excellence must begin privately or it will never show up when it counts.

---

4. Private Work Creates Public Advantage

Most people work only when necessary. CEOs work consistently, intentionally, and strategically. This private work creates a massive advantage because:

- You become sharper than others
- You become more prepared
- You increase your value
- You build deeper knowledge
- You develop rare discipline
- You become irreplaceable

While others waste time, you build power.

---

5. Private Habits Shape Your Identity

Leadership is not something you turn on and off—it's who you become.

Your private actions shape your identity more than anything else.

If you tell yourself you are disciplined, but your private habits prove otherwise, you weaken your self-image.

If you act like a leader only when watched, you create a shaky foundation.

But if you consistently act with strength, structure, and excellence in private, you naturally embody leadership everywhere you go.

Your identity follows your habits.

---

6. Private Leadership Protects You From External Pressure

When you lead yourself well in private, pressure cannot break you.

You are prepared.

You are trained.

You are stable.

You are confident because you know the work you put in behind the scenes.

This is why CEOs remain calm under fire—they didn't start practicing leadership in front of people. They built it in silence.

---

7. Self-Leadership Requires Self-Honesty

In private moments, you must be brutally honest with yourself:

- Did I give my best today?
- Did I avoid what I needed to face?
- Did I stay aligned with my goals?
- Did I push myself or hide from effort?
- Did I keep my promises?

Self-honesty builds growth. Self-deception destroys it.

---

8. Who You Are in Private Becomes Who You Are in Public

You cannot fake leadership.

You cannot fake discipline.

You cannot fake confidence.

You cannot fake character.

Your private actions eventually reveal themselves—good or bad.

If you want to lead others effectively, you must first lead yourself consistently.

---

9. The Strength You Build in Private Makes You Unshakeable

The quiet grind strengthens your mind.

The unseen effort strengthens your skills.

The personal discipline strengthens your character.

This is what creates undeniable presence, confidence, and influence.

People feel it when someone is truly a leader—it cannot be hidden.

Leading yourself when no one is watching is the highest form of leadership.

It is the foundation of excellence, the birthplace of character, and the source of true power.

When you master private leadership, your public success becomes guaranteed.

CHAPTER 15 — Decision-Making Under Uncertainty

A CEO's greatest skill isn't knowing the future—it's making strong decisions **without** knowing the future. Uncertainty is guaranteed. Risk is unavoidable. Pressure is constant. What separates high-level leaders from everyone else is their ability to choose wisely when the answers aren't clear, the information isn't complete, and the outcome isn't guaranteed.

Average performers freeze under uncertainty. They hesitate, overthink, procrastinate, or avoid choices altogether. CEOs move forward with clarity, confidence, and controlled judgment. They understand that **indecision is far more dangerous than the wrong decision**. Movement creates information. Hesitation creates doubt.

Decision-making under uncertainty is not luck. It is a learned skill, sharpened through discipline, awareness, and mental strength.

---

1. Accept That Certainty Is Rare

Most people wait for perfect clarity before they act. The problem?

Perfect clarity never comes.

There will always be unknowns.

There will always be risk.

There will always be factors you cannot control.

CEOs don't wait for the perfect moment—they create momentum by acting with the information they have. Progress comes from movement, not waiting.

---

2. Focus on Controllables

In uncertain situations, the mind tries to worry about everything at once. This creates overwhelm and paralysis. CEOs cut through confusion by focusing strictly on what they can control:

- Their mindset
- Their effort
- Their actions
- Their preparation
- Their next step

Everything else is noise.

By controlling the controllables, uncertainty becomes manageable.

---

3. Gather Information Quickly, Not Perfectly

Leaders don't guess—they investigate.

But they do it efficiently.

A CEO gathers enough information to make an informed decision, but they do not drown in details. They understand that too much information is just as dangerous as too little. Their goal is clarity, not perfection.

Ask yourself:

- What do I know for sure?
- What information do I actually need?
- What assumptions am I making?
- What does the data suggest?

Once you have the essentials, you move.

---

4. Use Principles, Not Emotions

Emotional decisions are unstable.

Principle-based decisions are strong.

CEOs base choices on:

- Long-term goals
- Core values
- Logic
- Risk assessment
- Strategic alignment

They don't let fear, frustration, or doubt cloud judgment.

Emotion may whisper, but principles decide.

---

5. Think in Probabilities, Not Guarantees

Nothing in leadership is guaranteed. CEOs make decisions by assessing **probabilities**:

- What's the most likely outcome?
- What is the upside potential?
- What is the downside risk?
- What is the worst-case scenario—and can I handle it?

Thinking in probabilities allows you to move without fear.

---

6. Make the Next Best Move

When the big picture feels overwhelming, CEOs narrow their focus and ask:

"What is the next best move I can make?"

Not the perfect move.

Not the final move.

The next best move.

This keeps momentum alive and prevents paralysis.

---

7. Stay Calm Under Pressure

Clarity requires emotional control.

Chaos destroys decision-making.

High-performance leaders bring calm into uncertainty by:

- Slowing their breathing
- Lowering their voice
- Thinking before speaking
- Asking clarifying questions
- Staying grounded in facts

Your calmness becomes your competitive advantage.

---

8. Make Decisions with Confidence

Even when uncertain, CEOs make decisions with authority.

Why?

Because confidence influences outcomes.

A hesitant decision creates hesitant results.

A firm decision creates firm action.

Confidence is not arrogance—it is commitment.

---

9. Reinforce with Fast Feedback

After making a decision, CEOs immediately evaluate:

- What worked?
- What didn't?
- What needs adjustment?

Feedback transforms uncertainty into improvement.

The more decisions you make, the stronger your decision-making becomes.

---

10. Trust Your Ability to Figure It Out

This is the mindset that transforms leaders:

"I may not know the full path, but I know I can handle whatever comes."

This belief turns uncertainty from something scary into something empowering.

You don't need perfect answers.

You need confidence in yourself.

Decision-making under uncertainty is not about predicting the future.

It is about navigating it with strength, logic, and purpose.

When you master this skill, you become fearless—not because the path is clear, but because you trust yourself to walk it with power.

This is the mindset of a CEO.

This is the mindset of a leader who cannot be shaken.

CHAPTER 16 — Mastering Self-Control & Focus

Self-control is the ability to govern your emotions, thoughts, and behaviors. Focus is the skill of directing your attention toward what truly matters. Together, they form one of the most powerful combinations in leadership. CEOs excel because they master both. They don't allow impulses, distractions, or emotions to dictate their actions. They move with intention, discipline, and clarity.

In a world full of noise, temptation, and constant demands, self-control and focus have become rare—but that's exactly why they create such an advantage. Most people drift. Leaders direct. Most people react. CEOs respond. Most people get pulled in a hundred directions. High-level thinkers stay locked in on what matters most.

Self-control is not about restriction. It's about protection—protecting your energy, your time, your mind, and your mission. Focus is not about intensity. It's about alignment—making sure your daily actions move you toward your long-term goals.

---

1. Self-Control Begins with Self-Awareness

You cannot control what you are unaware of.

To control yourself, you must understand yourself:

- What triggers you?
- What distracts you?
- What drains your energy?
- What environments make you unfocused?
- What emotions lead you into bad decisions?

CEOs study these patterns.

Because once you know your tendencies, you can master them.

---

2. Emotions Must Follow Purpose, Not Lead It

Emotions are powerful—but they cannot be the driver.

Anger, fear, excitement, frustration, pressure—these emotions will always appear.

The question is: **Do you act from emotion or from purpose?**

People who react emotionally make impulsive, short-sighted decisions.

CEOs pause, process, and choose logically.

Self-control allows you to remain stable while others fall apart.

---

3. Focus Is a Discipline, Not a Feeling

Most people wait to "feel focused."

High-level leaders create focus.

They do this by:

- Eliminating distractions
- Setting clear priorities
- Working in structured blocks
- Protecting their environment
- Saying NO to anything misaligned
- Giving each task their full attention

You don't find focus—you build it.

---

4. Control Your Environment or It Will Control You

Your environment shapes your behavior more than your willpower does.

You cannot stay focused in a chaotic, distracting, or negative environment.

CEOs engineer their surroundings by:

- Removing unnecessary noise
- Keeping their workspace clean

- Surrounding themselves with driven people
- Limiting social media and digital distractions
- Creating order so their mind can think clearly

A focused environment produces a focused mind.

---

5. Master the Art of Pausing

Self-control doesn't mean suppressing emotions.

It means pausing long enough to choose the best response.

Before reacting, ask:

- "What outcome do I want?"
- "Does this reaction move me closer or further?"
- "Is this a moment to respond or a moment to be silent?"

That one pause can protect relationships, prevent mistakes, and maintain clarity.

---

6. Focus on What Moves the Needle

Not all tasks are equal.

Not all responsibilities matter.

Not everything deserves your energy.

High-level leaders prioritize only the tasks that create real progress.

They ask:

- "What is the ONE thing that matters most right now?"
- "What action will produce the biggest result?"
- "What is the smartest way to use my energy?"

Focus on the vital few, not the trivial many.

---

7. Remove the Distraction of Multitasking

Multitasking is a myth.

Your brain cannot focus deeply on multiple things at once.

When you split your attention, you reduce your clarity, quality, and speed.

CEOs choose **single-task dominance**:

One task.

One focus.

One intention.

One outcome.

Deep focus is a competitive advantage.

---

8. Build Focus Through Habits, Not Force

You cannot rely on willpower every day.

You need structured routines that automatically create focus:

- Morning clarity rituals
- Pre-work mental reset
- Time-blocked work sessions
- Scheduled breaks
- Daily priority lists
- Evening reflection

Habits create consistency.

Consistency creates mastery.

---

9. Protect Your Energy Like a Valuable Asset

You cannot lead well if your mind is drained.

You cannot stay focused if your energy is scattered.

High performers protect their energy by:

- Resting strategically
- Managing stress proactively
- Eating and sleeping well
- Avoiding draining people

- Setting firm boundaries

A focused leader is an energized leader.

---

10. Self-Control Creates Freedom

People think self-control restricts you.

In reality, it liberates you.

When you control your impulses, you gain:

- Freedom from distraction
- Freedom from emotional chaos
- Freedom from inconsistency
- Freedom from regret
- Freedom to stay aligned with your goals

Focus and self-control give you your life back.

Mastering self-control and focus doesn't make life easier—it makes *you* stronger.

It gives you clarity when others are confused.

It gives you composure when others are emotional.

It gives you direction when others are scattered.

This is the mindset of a CEO:

Calm.

Intentional.

Focused.

Disciplined.

Unshakeable.

CHAPTER 17 — How CEOs Manage Stress & Chaos

Stress is unavoidable. Chaos is inevitable. Pressure is constant.

But while most people crumble under these conditions, CEOs learn to operate at their *best* when environments become unstable. They don't avoid stress—they manage it. They don't run from chaos—they organize it. And they don't collapse under pressure—they rise.

A CEO's job requires emotional control, mental clarity, and consistent leadership through uncertainty. This chapter reveals how top leaders stay grounded, focused, and effective no matter how intense the situation becomes.

Stress doesn't break CEOs—it sharpens them.

---

1. They Stay Calm When Others Panic

When chaos hits, most people react emotionally. They complain, blame, freeze, or spiral.

CEOs do the opposite—they remain calm.

This calmness isn't natural; it's trained.

They breathe.

They observe.

They slow down their tone.

They analyze before acting.

A calm leader brings order to chaos.

Your emotional state becomes the emotional state of your environment.

---

2. They Prioritize What Truly Matters

Chaos makes everything feel urgent.

Stress makes every problem feel bigger than it is.

High-level leaders cut through the noise by asking:

- "What actually matters right now?"
- "What is the real problem I need to solve?"
- "What can wait?"
- "What deserves my full focus?"

This ability to filter chaos turns overwhelming situations into manageable tasks.

Clarity eliminates panic.

---

3. They Control Their Breathing and Body Language

Stress affects the body first:

- Your heart rate increases
- Your breath shortens
- Your muscles tighten
- Your mind speeds up

CEOs use physiological control to regulate emotional control.

A calm body supports a calm mind.

Simple techniques include:

- Deep breathing
- Slowed speech
- Relaxed posture
- Controlled gestures

Your body language influences your mental clarity.

---

4. They Create Structure Inside Chaos

Chaos thrives when there is no structure.

Leadership begins by creating order.

CEOs quickly establish:

- Priorities
- Roles

- Timelines
- Procedures
- Next steps

Structure reduces fear because it replaces uncertainty with direction.

---

5. They Don't Try to Control Everything

People feel overwhelmed because they try to manage things they cannot influence.

CEOs only focus on:

- What they can control
- What they can influence
- What they must accept

By letting go of what is outside their reach, they preserve their energy for what truly matters.

Stress decreases when control becomes strategic.

---

6. They Ask the Right Questions

In chaotic moments, the wrong questions create confusion.

The right questions create clarity.

CEOs ask:

- "What is the real root of this situation?"
- "What is the smartest response?"
- "What options do we have?"
- "What is the worst-case scenario—and how do we prevent it?"
- "How do we turn this into an opportunity?"

Questions slice through emotional fog.

---

7. They Break Problems Into Small, Solvable Parts

Stress becomes overwhelming when the mind sees a problem as one huge block.

CEOs break challenges into steps:

- What needs attention first?
- What is step one?
- What resources are required?
- Who can help?

Small actions eliminate big anxiety.

---

8. They Maintain Emotional Boundaries

Leaders absorb pressure—but they do not internalize it.

They stay emotionally available without becoming emotionally overwhelmed.

They know:

- When to pause
- When to detach
- When to delegate
- When to rest
- When to protect their energy

A burned-out leader cannot guide anyone.

---

9. They Communicate With Clarity and Confidence

During stress, people look for reassurance.

They want leadership that is calm, confident, and direct.

CEOs use communication to:

- Reduce fear
- Provide direction
- Offer solutions
- Align people
- Restore stability

Clear communication is a stabilizing force.

---

10. They Treat Stress as a Teacher, Not an Enemy

Stress reveals weaknesses in:

- Systems
- Discipline
- Organization
- Communication
- Mindset

Instead of fearing stress, CEOs study it.

They ask:

- "What is this situation showing me?"
- "What can be improved?"
- "How can we prevent this in the future?"

Stress becomes a source of growth, not destruction.

---

11. They Use Recovery as a Strategic Tool

Even the strongest leaders require rest.

CEOs don't push endlessly—they recover intentionally through:

- Quiet time
- Reflection
- Limited screens
- Restorative sleep
- Working out
- Reconnecting with purpose

A recovered mind makes better decisions.

---

12. They Stay Solution-Focused

Stress makes people dwell on problems.

CEOs focus on solutions.

They shift their mindset from:

"What's going wrong?" → **"What do we need to solve?"**

“Who’s at fault?” → **“How do we fix this?”**

“This is terrible.” → **“What’s the opportunity here?”**

Solution-based thinking prevents emotional spirals.

CEOs don’t avoid stress—they manage it, channel it, and use it to become stronger.

They maintain clarity while others lose control.

They stay composed while others panic.

They act with purpose while others react with emotion.

This mastery over stress and chaos is what makes a leader unstoppable.

CHAPTER 18 — The Art of Adaptability

Adaptability is the ability to adjust, evolve, and respond effectively when circumstances change. In a world where nothing stays the same—markets shift, people shift, goals shift, environments shift—adaptability becomes one of the most valuable leadership skills a person can possess. CEOs thrive because they do not fear change… they *flow* with it.

Most people resist change. They cling to what's familiar, even when it's no longer working. They fear uncertainty and avoid anything that challenges their comfort. But CEOs understand that adaptability is the gateway to growth. The more flexible your mind is, the more powerful your decisions become.

Adaptability is not weakness.

It is not inconsistency.

It is not indecision.

Adaptability is strategic evolution.

---

1. Adaptability Begins With Acceptance

You cannot adapt to something you refuse to acknowledge.

People who struggle with change usually struggle with acceptance.

Acceptance means:

- Recognizing the reality of the situation
- Letting go of what no longer serves you
- Being willing to move forward
- Releasing emotional resistance

Accepting reality puts you in a position of power. Once you accept, you can adjust.

---

2. Adaptability Requires a Flexible Mindset

Rigidity is the enemy of growth.

Flexible thinkers stay open, curious, and aware.

A flexible mindset asks:

- "What's the opportunity here?"
- "What can I learn from this?"
- "How can I use this to my advantage?"
- "What's the smartest next move?"

When your mind remains open, solutions appear faster and clearer.

---

3. Adapt Quickly, Not Emotionally

Adaptability is not about reacting impulsively.

It's about adjusting intelligently.

Emotion leads to panic.

Adaptation requires clarity.

CEOs evaluate changes by asking:

- What just shifted?
- What does this mean?
- What needs to be updated?
- How do we reposition ourselves?

They do not freeze.

They do not deny.

They do not overreact.

They adapt with purpose.

---

4. They Don't Take Change Personally

Many people resist change because they take it as a personal attack:

- "Why is this happening to me?"
- "Why is everything going wrong?"

- “Why can’t things stay the same?”

CEOs remove ego from the equation.

They view change as information, not an insult.

As a signal, not a punishment.

This emotional neutrality keeps them grounded and effective.

---

5. They Pivot Without Losing the Mission

Adaptability doesn’t mean abandoning your goals.

It means adjusting your strategy so the mission *still* gets accomplished.

The vision stays the same.

The method evolves.

A CEO is not attached to the *how*.

They are committed to the *outcome*.

---

6. Adaptability Requires Curiosity, Not Fear

Fear closes the mind.

Curiosity opens it.

When faced with change, CEOs ask curious questions:

- “What can this teach me?”
- “What if this is actually an upgrade?”
- “How can I innovate through this?”

Curiosity turns fear into fuel.

---

7. They Prepare for Multiple Outcomes

Rigid thinkers only plan for one scenario.

CEOs plan for several.

They think forward:

- If Plan A fails → What’s Plan B?

- If the environment shifts → How do we adjust?
- If resources change → What systems stay strong?

This readiness keeps them steady when others fall apart.

---

8. They See Disruption as an Opportunity

Most people see disruption as loss.

Leaders see disruption as leverage.

Chaos opens doors that stability never reveals.

A recession can build new businesses.

A setback can ignite new skills.

A shift in the environment can highlight new leadership opportunities.

Adaptable leaders capitalize on these moments.

---

9. They Stay Emotionally Light

Adaptable leaders do not carry emotional weight.

They don't overthink.

They don't cling to past mistakes.

They don't let yesterday drain today.

Emotional lightness creates mental agility.

The lighter you feel internally, the easier you shift externally.

---

10. They Grow Through Change, Not Around It

Most people try to avoid change.

Leaders grow through it.

Every challenge teaches a skill.

Every shift sharpens awareness.

Every transition builds resilience.

Adaptability becomes a transformational process.

Adapting does not mean you are inconsistent.

It doesn't mean you're unsure.

It doesn't mean you're weak.

Adaptability means you can:

- Bend without breaking
- Shift without losing your identity
- Adjust without losing direction
- Evolve without losing purpose

This is why adaptable leaders rise quickly—they are prepared for anything.

They don't chase comfort.

They chase growth.

In a world that never stops changing, adaptability is the skill that keeps you relevant, resilient, and unstoppable.

CHAPTER 19 — Understanding Your Leadership Power

Leadership power is not about authority, position, or titles—it is about **influence**, **clarity**, and **the ability to move people and situations forward**. Many people underestimate their power because they associate leadership only with external recognition. But CEOs know that true leadership begins internally. It is built through confidence, character, consistency, and the belief that you can create impact.

Understanding your leadership power means understanding the effect you have on yourself, on others, and on the direction of your life. Every thought, action, decision, and standard you hold influences outcomes. Leadership is not something you "get"—it's something you **grow into**.

When you realize the power you carry, you begin to operate at a higher level.

---

1. Leadership Power Begins With Self-Influence

Before you can move others, you must be able to move yourself.

Self-influence means:

- Setting your own direction
- Holding yourself to high standards
- Motivating yourself without external pressure
- Maintaining discipline when no one is watching
- Speaking to yourself with strength, not doubt

If you cannot influence your own actions, thoughts, and habits, you cannot expect others to follow you.

Power starts internally.

---

2. Confidence Amplifies Your Leadership Presence

Your presence speaks before you do.

People feel your confidence—or the lack of it.

Leadership power grows when you:

- Trust your decisions
- Communicate with clarity
- Stand tall
- Make eye contact
- Control your energy
- Move with intention

Confidence is not loud.

Confidence is calm, grounded, and consistent.

A confident leader shifts environments without forcing anything.

---

3. Leadership Power Comes From Responsibility

People with leadership power do not avoid responsibility—they embrace it.

They take ownership of:

- Their actions
- Their results
- Their behavior
- Their choices
- Their consequences

Responsibility builds credibility.

Credibility builds trust.

Trust builds influence.

Influence is power.

---

4. You Influence People Through Behavior, Not Words

People listen to your words… but they follow your actions.

Leadership power grows when your behavior matches your message.

When people see you:

- Stay consistent
- Handle pressure well
- Communicate respectfully
- Finish what you start
- Keep your promises
- Show discipline
- Demonstrate emotional maturity

They naturally begin to follow your lead.

You don't have to force influence—your example creates it.

---

5. Leadership Power Requires Emotional Stability

People follow leaders who stay steady through chaos.

Your emotions set the tone.

When you stay:

- Calm under pressure
- Rational under stress
- Controlled during conflict
- Consistent during uncertainty

People view you as strong, reliable, and trustworthy.

Emotional stability is leadership power.

---

6. Your Standards Create Influence

Leadership is not built by how you treat people occasionally—it is built by the standards you live by daily.

Your standards tell people:

- What you will allow
- What you won't tolerate
- What you believe in

- What you expect from yourself
- What you expect from others

High standards create high respect.

Low standards create low influence.

Your standards speak for you.

---

7. Leadership Power Requires Purpose

Power without purpose is dangerous.

Purpose gives direction to your influence.

Purpose makes you:

- Resilient
- Disciplined
- Focused
- Consistent
- Vision-oriented

People follow leaders who lead with conviction.

Purpose makes your influence meaningful.

---

8. Your Leadership Power Comes From Impact, Not Control

Leadership is not about controlling people—it's about impacting them.

Impact is created by:

- Your values
- Your attitude
- Your work ethic
- Your communication
- Your empathy
- Your consistency

When people feel inspired, supported, understood, and motivated by you, your power expands naturally.

---

9. Leadership Power Requires Continuous Growth

You cannot lead at a high level if you stay the same.

CEOs constantly improve their:

- Skills
- Emotional intelligence
- Communication
- Decision-making
- Discipline
- Awareness

Growth expands your influence.

Influence expands your power.

Your leadership becomes stronger every time you elevate yourself.

---

10. Your Leadership Power Already Exists—You Must Activate It

You don't need permission to lead.

You don't need a title to lead.

You don't need validation to lead.

Leadership begins the moment you decide to:

- Take control of your life
- Operate with integrity
- Stand on your principles
- Set a positive example
- Influence through actions
- Improve others by improving yourself

Your power is already within you.

You simply have to use it.

Understanding your leadership power is understanding that you have the ability to shape your life, influence your environment, elevate others, and lead with purpose. When you embrace this power, you stop living passively and start living intentionally.

You begin to operate like a CEO of your life—clear, confident, disciplined, and impactful.

CHAPTER 20 — Crafting Your Personal CEO Code

(Expanded Version)

Every great CEO operates by a personal code—a set of standards, principles, and non-negotiable values that guide their actions, decisions, leadership style, and identity. This personal code becomes their internal compass. It keeps them disciplined, focused, and aligned even when the world becomes chaotic, stressful, or uncertain.

Most people live based on emotion.

CEOs live based on a code.

Your personal CEO code is the foundation of your leadership.

It defines *who you are*, *how you operate*, and *what you stand for*.

It shapes your habits, your discipline, your relationships, and your success.

Instead of reacting to life, you begin directing it.

---

1. What Is a Personal CEO Code?

A personal CEO code is a written (or mental) declaration of the standards and principles you refuse to compromise.

It is your rulebook for success.

It is your anchor when stress hits.

It is the identity you hold yourself accountable to.

Your code determines:

- How you handle adversity
- How you treat people
- How you make decisions
- How you lead yourself
- How consistent you become
- How high you rise

Without a code, you drift.

With a code, you dominate.

---

2. Your Code Begins With Your Identity

Before you write your code, ask yourself:

"Who am I becoming?"

Your identity shapes your code.

Your code shapes your decisions.

Your decisions shape your life.

Examples of identity-driven declarations:

- "I am disciplined."
- "I am a leader."
- "I am calm under pressure."
- "I am committed to excellence."
- "I am consistent no matter what."

Your code must align with the future version of you—not your past.

---

3. Define Your Non-Negotiable Standards

Every CEO has standards that they never bend, regardless of mood, environment, or circumstances.

Your standards may include:

- I do not quit.
- I keep my word.
- I finish what I start.
- I control my emotions.
- I do not make excuses.
- I treat people with respect.
- I operate with integrity.
- I stay consistent even when it's uncomfortable.

These rules become the backbone of your life.

---

4. Establish Your Leadership Principles

Your leadership principles define how you move through the world. They shape your character and your influence.

Examples:

- Lead by example, not just words.
- Stay accountable when things go wrong.
- Speak with honesty but never with disrespect.
- Make decisions based on logic, not emotion.
- Serve others while standing firm in your standards.

These principles help you lead yourself and others with clarity.

---

5. Create Personal Performance Rules

Performance rules guide your productivity, habits, and daily execution.

Examples:

- Start each day with intention.
- Eliminate distractions during work time.
- Protect your energy and mental clarity.
- Prioritize tasks that create real progress.
- Master time instead of being mastered by it.

These rules keep you consistent, organized, and effective.

---

6. Define Your Emotional Guidelines

Your emotions influence your leadership more than any skill. Your code must address emotional control.

Examples:

- Never react out of anger.
- Breathe before responding.
- Stay calm under pressure.
- Choose rationality over impulse.

- Turn setbacks into strategy.

These guidelines keep you grounded and respected.

---

7. Determine Your Long-Term Commitments

Your code should include commitments that hold your vision intact.

Examples:

- Commit to lifelong learning.
- Commit to becoming financially intelligent.
- Commit to maintaining your health and energy.
- Commit to breaking generational patterns.
- Commit to improving yourself every year.

These commitments future-proof your leadership.

---

8. Make Your Code Practical, Not Just Inspirational

A code must be lived—not just written.

CEOs integrate their code into daily life by:

- Reviewing it every morning
- Reflecting on it every night
- Using it to guide decisions
- Returning to it during stress
- Holding themselves accountable to it

Your code must be active and alive.

---

9. Your Code Must Be Unshakeable During Hard Times

Anyone can follow a standard when life is easy.

Your code becomes powerful when you follow it while:

- Tired
- Stressed
- Tempted
- Unmotivated

- Disappointed
- Under pressure

Your code must hold strong when everything else feels unstable.

---

10. Your Code Becomes Your Legacy

When you operate by a strong personal code:

- People trust you
- People respect you
- People follow you
- People depend on you
- People remember you

Your leadership becomes predictable, consistent, and admired.

Your code shapes your identity.

Your identity shapes your behavior.

Your behavior shapes your results.

Your results shape your legacy.

Crafting your personal CEO code is not about perfection—it's about direction.

It's about becoming intentional, powerful, and aligned.

It's about operating from strength instead of emotion.

Once you live by your code, your entire presence changes.

You move differently.

You think differently.

You lead differently.

You WIN differently.

Your code becomes the blueprint for who you are—and who you are becoming.

CHAPTER 21 — Communicating With Authority

Great leaders are defined by the way they communicate. Their words carry weight. Their presence commands respect. Their tone influences decisions. Their clarity eliminates confusion. CEOs understand that communication is not just about speaking—it's about **leading through language**.

Authority in communication doesn't mean being loud, aggressive, or dominating.

True authority is calm, measured, confident, and intentional. It is the ability to speak in a way that earns attention without demanding it.

Communication is power—when it is mastered.

---

1. Authority Begins With Your Presence

Before you speak, people read your energy.

Authority is conveyed through:

- Your posture
- Your eye contact
- Your calmness
- Your confidence
- Your silence
- Your control of the environment

When your presence is strong, your words land harder.

Authority is felt before it is heard.

---

2. Speak Clearly, Not Perfectly

People think authority requires perfect vocabulary or flawless grammar.

It doesn't.

Authority requires **clarity**, not perfection.

Clarity comes from:

- Speaking with intention
- Using simple, strong language
- Organizing your thoughts before speaking
- Getting to the point
- Eliminating filler words

When your communication is clear, people trust you.

---

3. Slow Your Speech to Increase Your Power

Rushed speech signals nervousness, insecurity, or lack of control.

Slowed speech signals confidence.

When you slow down:

- People listen more
- Your words feel more deliberate
- You appear in control
- You command the room

Powerful communicators never rush.

They understand the value of pacing.

---

4. Use Tone as a Leadership Tool

Your tone determines how your message is received.

A strong tone is:

- Calm
- Even
- Controlled
- Confident
- Grounded

A weak tone is:

- Emotional
- Unsteady

- Loud without purpose
- Nervous or defensive

Authority lives in your tone far more than your words.

---

5. Communicate With Intentional Silence

Silence is one of the most underrated leadership tools.

It creates impact.

Strategic silence helps you:

- Command attention
- Make your message land
- Control the pace of conversation
- Show confidence
- Think before responding
- Put pressure on the listener

People with authority are not afraid of silence.

They use it intelligently.

---

6. Keep Your Message Focused

Weak communicators talk too much.

Strong communicators say only what matters.

Authority grows when your message is:

- Direct
- Purposeful
- Easy to understand
- Free from emotional rambling

People respect leaders who communicate with precision.

---

7. Listen With the Intent to Lead

Authority doesn't only come from speaking—it comes from listening.

CEOs listen to:

- Understand, not react
- Identify the real issue
- Hear what people aren't saying
- Gather information before acting
- Strengthen relationships

When you listen deeply, your responses carry more weight.

---

8. Control Your Emotional Delivery

Emotion is natural, but emotional communication creates chaos.

Authority requires emotional discipline:

- No reacting out of anger
- No raising your voice unnecessarily
- No defensive explanations
- No passive-aggressive remarks

A leader's words must remain steady even when emotions run high.

---

9. Communicate Expectations, Not Assumptions

Weak communication creates confusion.

Confusion creates failure.

Strong leaders communicate:

- Clear expectations
- Clear timelines
- Clear responsibilities
- Clear consequences
- Clear standards

Authority grows when you eliminate ambiguity.

---

10. Speak From Logic, Not Ego

Authority is not arrogance.

Authority is clarity.

Ego destroys influence.

Logic reinforces it.

Logical communication is:

- Structured
- Evidence-based
- Thoughtful
- Strategic

This type of communication earns respect naturally.

---

11. Mean What You Say and Say What You Mean

People trust leaders whose words match their actions.

Authority collapses when you:

- Make empty promises
- Speak without follow-through
- Overcommit
- Underperform
- Change your stance constantly

Consistency strengthens your voice.

Your integrity strengthens your authority.

---

12. Communicate With the Future in Mind

Every word you say influences:

- How people perceive you
- How they respond to you
- How much they trust you
- Whether they follow your lead

Communicate like someone who understands the long-term impact of their voice.

Your communication is one of your greatest leadership tools.

When you speak with clarity, confidence, control, and purpose, people listen.

When you command your words, you command your environment.

Communication is not just a skill—it is a leadership advantage.

Master it, and your influence becomes unstoppable.

CHAPTER 22 — Building a High-Performance Mindset

(Expanded Version)

Success doesn't start with talent, resources, or opportunity—it starts with mindset. The way you think determines how far you go, how much you grow, and how consistently you perform. CEOs don't think like everyone else. They train their minds to operate at a higher level. They cultivate a mindset built on resilience, discipline, consistency, and relentless improvement.

A high-performance mindset is not about being perfect.

It's about being intentional.

It's about directing your thoughts instead of letting them control you.

It's about elevating your standards and refusing to drop them.

When you master your mindset, you master your performance—and your life.

---

1. High Performance Begins With Mental Discipline

Your mind is powerful, but without discipline it becomes unfocused, emotional, and reactive.

High performers train their minds the same way athletes train their bodies.

Mental discipline includes:

- Controlling your thoughts
- Redirecting negative thinking
- Staying focused on solutions
- Refusing to indulge excuses
- Keeping your emotions in check
- Maintaining clarity under pressure

Discipline gives your mind structure.

Structure gives your life direction.

---

2. Eliminate the "Average Mindset"

Most people operate with limiting beliefs like:

- "I can't do it."
- "I don't know how."
- "I'm tired."
- "This is too hard."
- "I'll try again later."

A high-performance mindset replaces these with:

- "I'll figure it out."
- "I can handle this."
- "One step at a time."
- "Let's get it done."
- "I don't wait for motivation—I create it."

High performers think in possibilities, not barriers.

---

3. Focus on Progress, Not Perfection

Perfection paralyzes people.

Progress moves people forward.

A high-performance mindset understands:

- Improvement is more important than perfection
- Small steps create big results
- Consistency beats intensity
- Failure is feedback, not defeat

Progress is the cornerstone of sustainable success.

---

4. Repetition Builds Mastery

You don't rise to the level of your goals—you rise to the level of your habits.

High performers repeat the fundamentals until they become automatic.

They know mastery doesn't come from doing something once—it comes from doing it repeatedly.

Repetition builds:

- Confidence
- Competence
- Speed
- Precision
- Consistency

Your habits shape your future.

---

5. Replace Emotion With Strategy

Average minds react emotionally.

High-performance minds respond strategically.

When something goes wrong, they ask:

- "What's the strategy here?"
- "What's the best move?"
- "What outcome do I want?"
- "How do I turn this into an advantage?"

Strategy gives you control.

Emotion gives the situation control.

---

6. Embrace Controlled Pressure

Pressure reveals your mindset.

It shows whether you rise or retreat.

High performers view pressure as:

- A sharpening tool
- A growth opportunity
- A test of readiness

- A chance to build resilience

Pressure doesn't break them—pressure polishes them.

---

7. Build Mental Toughness Through Challenges

Mental toughness grows through resistance, not comfort.

Every challenge trains your mind to become stronger.

You build toughness when you:

- Push yourself when it's uncomfortable
- Stay disciplined on hard days
- Keep going when your emotions say stop
- Focus when others get distracted
- Find solutions when others complain

Toughness is built, not gifted.

---

8. Surround Yourself With High-Performance Influences

Your environment shapes your mindset.

If you are surrounded by negativity, excuses, or low standards, your mind will mirror it.

High performers intentionally choose environments filled with:

- Driven people
- High standards
- Growth-focused conversations
- Mentors and role models
- Accountability
- Encouragement and challenge

Your circle determines your ceiling.

---

9. Celebrate Wins, Learn From Losses

A high-performance mindset does not fear failure.

It uses failure as feedback.

High performers ask after every outcome:

- "What did I learn?"
- "What can I refine?"
- "How can I do this better next time?"
- "What worked—and why?"

Reflection turns experience into wisdom.

---

10. Commit to Lifelong Growth

High performers are always evolving.

They never reach a point where they stop improving.

They read.

They study.

They experiment.

They invest in themselves.

They learn new skills.

They upgrade their mindset continuously.

Growth keeps your performance sharp.

A high-performance mindset makes you unstoppable.

It elevates your thinking, sharpens your focus, and strengthens your discipline.

It turns ordinary effort into extraordinary results.

When you think like a high performer, you operate like a CEO—calm, focused, strategic, resilient, and committed to constant evolution.

CHAPTER 23 — Decision Velocity: Making Smart Choices Fast

(Expanded Version)

In leadership, speed matters.

Opportunities don't wait.

Problems don't pause.

Life doesn't slow down so you can think.

CEOs succeed because they make **smart decisions quickly**—a skill known as **decision velocity**.

Decision velocity is not rushing.

It is not guessing.

It is not acting recklessly.

Decision velocity is the ability to assess a situation, filter the noise, choose the best option, and move with confidence—without hesitation or fear.

Most people overthink.

Leaders **decide, act, adjust, and advance**.

Decision velocity is one of the most powerful advantages you can develop.

---

1. Overthinking Slows Down Your Success

Overthinking is the killer of momentum.

It creates:

- Self-doubt
- Confusion
- Emotional paralysis
- Missed opportunities
- Unnecessary fear

The longer you think, the harder it becomes to move.

High-level performers don't waste time in mental loops.

They gather what they need, eliminate what they don't, and take action.

---

2. Decision Velocity Requires Simplicity

Complicated thinking slows you down.

Leaders simplify.

They ask simple, powerful questions:

- "What outcome do I want?"
- "What are my top two options?"
- "What's the smartest next step?"
- "What is the risk—and can I handle it?"

Clear questions create fast decisions.

---

3. Separate Emotion From Evaluation

Emotion clouds judgment.

Logic clarifies it.

Before deciding, CEOs quickly identify:

- What is emotional?
- What is factual?
- What assumptions am I making?
- What bias is influencing me?

Once emotion is removed, the right choice becomes obvious.

---

4. Use the 70% Rule

Great leaders rarely have 100% of the information.

They move at **70% clarity**, because:

- Perfect certainty doesn't exist

- Waiting too long becomes a liability
- Momentum is more valuable than perfection

If something has a 70% chance of working, they move.

Then they adjust as they go.

---

5. Choose Direction Over Perfection

People waste months trying to make the perfect decision.

CEOs know:

A good decision made now is better than a perfect decision made too late.

Movement creates clarity.

Clarity creates adjustment.

Adjustment creates success.

Perfection is the enemy of decision velocity.

---

6. Break Choices Into Small Steps

Big decisions create mental pressure.

Leaders break them down.

Instead of asking, "What's the best final decision?" they ask:

- "What is step one?"
- "What do I need right now—not later?"

Small steps reduce stress and accelerate action.

---

7. Identify the Fastest Path to Impact

When making decisions, CEOs don't choose what feels good—they choose what moves the needle.

They ask:

- "Which option creates the biggest result?"
- "Which option gets us closer to the goal fastest?"

- "Which option saves time and energy?"

Decision velocity requires prioritizing impact over emotion.

---

8. Use Data, Not Guesswork

Even fast decisions require input.

Smart leaders use:

- Past results
- Key metrics
- Trends
- Patterns
- Expert feedback
- Their own experience

Good data + fast judgment = strong decisions.

---

9. Trust Your Preparation

Confidence in decision-making doesn't come from knowing everything—it comes from knowing **you're prepared**.

When you consistently:

- Study
- Reflect
- Stay aware
- Build experience
- Strengthen your discipline

Your instincts become sharp and reliable.

Preparation builds decision speed.

---

10. Make the Decision, Then Commit

A weak decision is one you keep revisiting.

Once a CEO decides:

- They commit

- They take action
- They communicate clearly
- They execute
- They adjust along the way

You cannot lead with hesitation.

You lead through commitment.

---

11. Use Feedback as Fuel, Not Judgment

Decision velocity improves over time.

After each major choice, leaders ask:

- "Did the decision create the outcome I wanted?"
- "What can be improved next time?"
- "Where did I hesitate—and why?"

This reflection turns decisions into lessons.

Lessons turn into speed.

Speed turns into mastery.

---

12. Decision Velocity Builds Unstoppable Confidence

When you make strong decisions quickly, you:

- Build trust in yourself
- Gain respect from others
- Increase your momentum
- Multiply your opportunities
- Upgrade your leadership presence

Indecision drains power.

Fast, intelligent decisions **create power**.

Decision velocity separates leaders from followers.

It turns pressure into clarity.

It transforms uncertainty into action.

It makes you efficient, strategic, and unstoppable.

When you make decisions fast—and make adjustments faster—you become a leader who moves the world forward instead of waiting on it.

CHAPTER 24 — Emotional Intelligence for Leaders

Emotional intelligence (EQ) is one of the most powerful leadership skills in the world. CEOs are not great because they know everything—they are great because they understand **people**, **emotions**, and **how to navigate human behavior with awareness and control**.

Where IQ measures knowledge, EQ measures **impact**.

IQ helps you solve problems.

EQ helps you lead people.

A leader with emotional intelligence is calm under pressure, aware of their own emotions, sensitive to the emotions of others, and able to communicate with clarity instead of conflict. EQ turns leaders into influencers, problem-solvers, negotiators, and stabilizers.

If you want to lead effectively, EQ is not optional—it is foundational.

---

1. Emotional Intelligence Begins With Self-Awareness

You cannot manage emotions you don't recognize.

Self-awareness means understanding:

- What triggers your frustration
- What increases your stress
- What drains your energy
- What motivates you
- What insecurities influence your reactions
- How your tone affects others
- How you show up under pressure

High-EQ leaders monitor their internal world with honesty—not judgment.

Awareness gives you control.

---

2. You Must Control Your Emotions Before Leading Others

People follow emotional stability.

They trust leaders who stay grounded.

Leaders with EQ:

- Don't react impulsively
- Don't take things personally
- Don't let frustration dictate their tone
- Don't blow up when stressed
- Don't allow fear to make decisions

Instead, they manage their emotions with maturity.

Emotional control creates leadership credibility.

---

3. EQ Makes You an Effective Communicator

Most communication problems come from emotional misunderstanding, not lack of words.

Leaders with emotional intelligence communicate by:

- Listening before responding
- Asking clarifying questions
- Speaking with empathy
- Reading tone and body language
- Staying calm in difficult conversations

When emotions stay controlled, conversations become productive instead of chaotic.

---

4. EQ Strengthens Relationships and Trust

People will work harder for leaders who understand them.

Emotional intelligence allows you to:

- Connect with people genuinely
- Build trust
- Understand different personalities

- Support others effectively
- Resolve conflicts without aggression
- Inspire loyalty through respect

Relationship-building is leadership currency.

---

5. EQ Helps You Read the Room

Great leaders don't just see situations—they feel them.

EQ allows you to sense:

- Tension
- Confusion
- Low morale
- Frustration
- Disengagement
- Motivation
- Unspoken issues

Being able to read the emotional climate helps you act before problems grow.

---

6. Use Empathy as a Leadership Tool

Empathy is not weakness.

Empathy is awareness.

Empathy means:

- Understanding someone's perspective
- Recognizing their challenges
- Listening without judgment
- Responding thoughtfully
- Showing respect

Empathy creates connection.

Connection creates influence.

---

7. EQ Helps You Manage Conflict Professionally

Conflict is natural.

Emotionally intelligent leaders handle it with control and clarity.

They don't:

- Argue
- Attack
- Escalate
- Get defensive

They instead:

- Listen
- De-escalate
- Clarify the issue
- Focus on solutions
- Maintain composure

High-EQ leaders turn conflict into alignment, not division.

---

8. EQ Supports Strong Decision-Making

Emotional chaos leads to poor decisions.

Emotional clarity leads to strong ones.

Emotionally intelligent leaders separate:

- Facts from feelings
- Logic from impulse
- Principle from emotion

This ability creates strategic decision-making even during stress.

---

9. EQ Makes You a Better Listener

Most people listen to respond.

Leaders with EQ listen to understand.

They listen for:

- Emotions behind words
- What is not being said
- The true root of the problem
- The intention behind the message

Listening creates understanding.

Understanding creates influence.

---

10. EQ Does Not Mean You Avoid Tough Conversations

Emotionally intelligent leaders do not shy away from accountability or difficult discussions.

They simply conduct them with professionalism.

EQ allows you to:

- Address performance issues without disrespect
- Set firm boundaries without anger
- Give feedback without attacking character
- Correct behavior while protecting relationships

This balance is what makes leadership sustainable.

---

11. EQ Helps You Stay Centered in Chaos

When environments get stressful, most people lose control.

Leaders with high EQ become more focused.

They:

- Breathe
- Stay grounded
- Think clearly
- Respond intelligently
- Maintain emotional stability

Their calmness becomes the anchor in chaotic moments.

---

12. Growing EQ Makes You Impossible to Shake

As your emotional intelligence increases:

- You become harder to intimidate
- Harder to manipulate
- Harder to provoke
- Harder to distract
- Harder to mislead

You gain control over yourself—and that gives you control over every environment you lead.

Emotional intelligence is the heart of leadership.

It gives you the power to influence, inspire, guide, and unify people with clarity and strength.

It makes you a leader others want to follow—not because they fear you, but because they respect you.

A leader with high EQ is powerful, intentional, and unshakeable.

CHAPTER 25 — Building Trust and Credibility

Trust and credibility are the foundation of all great leadership. Without trust, people won't follow you. Without credibility, people won't believe you. CEOs know that trust isn't given—it's earned through consistent behavior, aligned actions, integrity, and reliability. Trust is built slowly, but it can be destroyed instantly.

Leadership is not just about authority—it's about *believability*.

People believe in leaders who behave with consistency, honesty, competence, and accountability. When your words match your actions, your credibility grows. When your actions contradict your words, your influence disappears.

Building trust and credibility is one of the most important investments a leader can make.

---

1. Trust Begins With Consistency

People trust what they can predict.

If they can't predict you, they can't trust you.

Consistency builds trust through:

- Showing up every day
- Keeping your promises
- Staying disciplined
- Maintaining your standards
- Being reliable regardless of mood

When people know what to expect from you, they feel secure around you.

Consistency is credibility.

---

2. Say What You Mean and Mean What You Say

Credibility collapses when your words don't align with your actions.

Leaders with integrity:

- Don't make empty promises
- Don't overcommit
- Don't agree to things they won't deliver
- Don't talk big and act small

They communicate honestly, even when it's difficult.

Your word must be your bond.

---

3. Follow Through Relentlessly

The fastest way to earn credibility is simple: **deliver**.

People respect leaders who:

- Finish what they start
- Meet deadlines
- Show up prepared
- Execute consistently
- Keep commitments even when it's inconvenient

Follow-through builds reputation.

Reputation builds trust.

---

4. Be Transparent, Not Perfect

People don't need you to be perfect—they need you to be honest.

Transparency builds trust because it shows authenticity.

Leaders earn respect when they:

- Acknowledge mistakes
- Admit what they don't know
- Communicate openly
- Explain their decisions
- Share their thought process

Transparency eliminates confusion and suspicion.

---

5. Own Your Mistakes Immediately

Weak leaders hide mistakes.

Strong leaders own them.

Accountability sounds like:

- "That was my fault."
- "Here's what I'm doing to fix it."
- "This won't happen again."

Owning your mistakes increases trust because it shows maturity and responsibility.

People don't expect perfection—

they expect honesty and correction.

---

6. Keep Your Standards High

People trust leaders who hold themselves to higher standards than they expect from others.

High standards show:

- Integrity
- Discipline
- Honor
- Respect
- Leadership strength

You cannot demand from others what you don't practice yourself.

Your standards become your credibility.

---

7. Communicate With Respect at All Times

Credibility evaporates when a leader communicates with disrespect, aggression, or emotional instability.

Respectful communication includes:

- Listening fully
- Not interrupting
- Speaking calmly
- Offering clarity, not confusion
- Communicating boundaries without hostility

Respect earns loyalty.

Disrespect erodes trust.

---

8. Be Competent and Prepared

People trust leaders who know what they're doing.

Competence builds confidence.

Competence means:

- Understanding your responsibilities
- Preparing before meetings
- Keeping your skills sharp
- Studying your craft
- Staying informed
- Being reliable under pressure

Competence + consistency = credibility.

---

9. Protect Confidential Information

Leaders earn trust by being trustworthy.

That means:

- Keeping private conversations private
- Never gossiping
- Never exposing someone's mistakes publicly
- Maintaining confidentiality like a professional

If people feel unsafe around you, they will never follow you.

---

10. Treat Everyone With Fairness

Credibility increases when you treat people equitably.

Favoritism destroys trust.

Fair leadership means:

- Making unbiased decisions
- Recognizing effort consistently
- Enforcing rules equally
- Valuing everyone's contributions

Fairness builds respect, and respect builds loyalty.

---

11. Be Predictable in Your Reactions

Nothing destroys trust like emotional unpredictability.

When people don't know:

- How you'll react
- What mood you'll be in
- Whether you'll stay calm or explode

…they stop trusting you.

Predictable emotional behavior increases stability.

Stability increases credibility.

---

12. Lead With Long-Term Integrity

Credibility is built through years of actions and moments of accountability.

You stay credible when you:

- Do the right thing when no one is watching
- Refuse shortcuts
- Keep your ethics strong
- Speak truthfully
- Stay disciplined under pressure

Your integrity is your greatest leadership asset.

Trust and credibility are not optional—they are essential.
Without them, leadership collapses.
With them, your influence becomes powerful, respected, and long-lasting.
A credible leader doesn't need to demand authority—
their actions earn it for them.

CHAPTER 26 — Managing People With Strength and Respect

Leadership is not about being above people—it's about elevating them.

Great CEOs manage people with a powerful balance of **strength and respect**. Too much strength without respect becomes intimidation. Too much respect without strength becomes weakness. True leadership requires both.

People don't follow titles—they follow leaders who know how to guide, support, challenge, and empower them. Managing people effectively means creating an environment where expectations are clear, standards are high, accountability is consistent, and every person feels valued and respected.

When you master this balance, you create teams that are loyal, motivated, and high-performing.

---

1. Strength Means Clarity, Not Aggression

Leaders often confuse strength with dominance.

Real strength is clarity.

Strong leaders:

- Set clear expectations
- Communicate directly
- Define roles and responsibilities
- Establish standards
- Hold people accountable

Aggression is emotional.

Strength is intentional.

---

2. Respect Means Seeking to Understand

People feel respected when they feel understood.

Respect in leadership includes:

- Listening fully without interruption
- Asking questions to understand their perspective
- Treating everyone with dignity
- Being fair and unbiased
- Acknowledging their contributions

Respect builds trust.

Trust builds influence.

---

3. Set High Standards—and Enforce Them Consistently

High-performing teams are created through consistent standards.

Effective leaders:

- Communicate the standard clearly
- Reinforce it regularly
- Lead by example
- Hold everyone accountable—no exceptions
- Correct behavior professionally

People respect leaders who enforce standards fairly and consistently.

---

4. Accountability Is a Form of Respect

Weak leaders avoid holding people accountable because they fear conflict.

Strong leaders address issues early because accountability creates growth.

Accountability sounds like:

- "This is what needs improvement."
- "Here's what I expect next time."
- "Let's correct this now before it becomes a bigger issue."

Holding someone accountable shows you believe they are capable of more.

---

5. Never Manage Through Fear

Fear produces short-term obedience but long-term resentment.

People may listen to a fearful leader, but they will never trust them.

Leadership through fear creates:

- High turnover
- Low morale
- Toxic environments
- Minimal creativity
- Disconnected teams

Real leaders inspire excellence—not fear.

---

6. Give Clear Direction, Not Confusing Instructions

Confusion leads to mistakes.

Clarity leads to action.

Strong leaders give direction that is:

- Specific
- Organized
- Easy to understand
- Focused on outcomes
- Delivered with confidence

When people know exactly what is expected, they perform at higher levels.

---

7. Use Strength to Protect the Team, Not Control Them

Your strength must work *for* your team, not against them.

Strength protects by:

- Setting boundaries

- Removing obstacles
- Standing up for your people
- Eliminating toxic behavior
- Providing structure and stability

People feel safe under strong leadership.

---

8. Give Feedback That Builds, Not Breaks

Feedback is essential for growth—

but the delivery determines its impact.

Effective feedback is:

- Direct but respectful
- Firm but empathetic
- Honest but supportive
- Focused on improvement, not criticism

People improve when they feel safe, not attacked.

---

9. Recognize and Reward Good Performance

People work harder when their effort is acknowledged.

Recognition can be:

- Verbal appreciation
- Public acknowledgment
- Added responsibility
- Growth opportunities
- Bonuses or incentives

Respect is shown through appreciation.

Appreciation builds loyalty.

---

10. Manage People Based on Their Strengths

Not everyone works the same way.

High-level leaders understand people individually.

This includes knowing:

- Their strengths
- Their weaknesses
- Their motivations
- Their work style
- Their communication preferences

Managing people individually increases team effectiveness.

---

11. Stay Emotionally Consistent

Nothing creates instability like a leader whose mood changes daily.

Strong leaders stay:

- Calm
- Steady
- Predictable
- Professional
- Emotionally controlled

People trust leaders who are emotionally consistent.

---

12. Lead With Humility, Not Ego

Respect grows when leaders stay grounded.

Humble leaders:

- Admit mistakes
- Ask for input
- Value other opinions
- Learn from their team
- Give credit freely

Humility attracts loyalty.

Ego destroys it.

Managing people with strength and respect is the hallmark of exceptional leadership.

It creates an environment where people feel supported, challenged, valued, and empowered.

When people feel respected, they perform at their highest level.

When people see your strength, they trust your leadership.

The combination of both makes you unstoppable.

CHAPTER 27 — Delegation: Trusting Others to Carry the Mission

A CEO's power doesn't come from doing everything themselves—it comes from empowering others to execute effectively. Delegation is not a sign of weakness. It is a sign of strength, trust, and strategic leadership.

Most people struggle with delegation because they think:

- "I can do it faster."
- "No one will do it like me."
- "I don't want mistakes."
- "I'll lose control."

But CEOs understand that doing everything alone limits growth.

Delegation multiplies your impact.

It expands your reach.

It develops your people.

It frees you to focus on high-level priorities.

When you trust others to carry the mission, the mission can grow beyond you.

---

1. Delegation Begins With Letting Go of Control

Leaders who try to control everything eventually burn out.

They become overwhelmed, stressed, and ineffective.

Delegation requires the belief:

"I don't have to do everything. I just have to lead everything."

Letting go doesn't mean losing control—

it means shifting from doing to directing.

---

2. Delegate Based on Strengths, Not Convenience

People thrive when they are assigned tasks aligned with their strengths.

Effective delegation requires asking:

- Who is best suited for this?
- Who has the skill?
- Who has the potential?
- Who can grow from this assignment?
- Who will be committed to the outcome?

Delegation becomes powerful when the right person gets the right task.

---

3. Communicate the Mission Clearly

Delegation fails when instructions are unclear.

A CEO explains:

- The objective
- The purpose
- The expected outcome
- The timeline
- The standards
- The resources available
- The boundaries

Clarity ensures execution.

Confusion creates mistakes.

---

4. Empower People Instead of Micromanaging Them

Micromanagement kills initiative, creativity, and confidence.

Delegation thrives when people feel trusted.

Empowerment looks like:

- Giving autonomy
- Allowing people to decide HOW to complete the task
- Providing support without suffocating

- Trusting their judgment
- Encouraging problem-solving

Trust builds ownership.

Ownership builds performance.

---

5. Set Check-In Points, Not Constant Monitoring

You don't need to hover.

You need structure.

Check-ins help you:

- Stay informed
- Offer guidance
- Provide feedback
- Ensure progress
- Prevent failures early

Structured check-ins maintain accountability without micromanagement.

---

6. Provide the Tools for Success

Delegation requires giving people what they need to win:

- Training
- Resources
- Information
- Access
- Direction
- Support

You cannot demand high performance from someone who is under-equipped.

---

7. Allow Room for Mistakes

Mistakes are not failures—they are part of development.

CEOs understand:

- People learn through execution
- Growth happens through experience
- Skills improve through practice

Instead of punishing mistakes, leaders use them as lessons.

Correct, don't criticize.

Coach, don't condemn.

---

8. Give Credit Generously

When the team wins, the credit goes to them.

When something goes wrong, the responsibility goes to the leader.

Celebrating your people strengthens morale and loyalty.

A strong leader says:

- "They did an excellent job."
- "Our success is because of the team."
- "I'm proud of how they executed."

Recognition motivates people to give even more.

---

9. Delegate to Build Leaders, Not Just Workers

Delegation is not just about completing tasks—

it's about growing people.

When you delegate:

- You expand their skills
- You increase their confidence
- You prepare them for bigger responsibilities
- You develop future leaders

The best CEOs build strong teams by developing strong individuals.

---

10. Focus on Outcomes, Not Methods

Effective delegation gives freedom in execution.

People may not complete tasks the way you would—and that's okay.

Your priority is the outcome, not the method.

Leaders communicate:

"This is the result I expect.

You choose the smartest way to get there."

Autonomy improves performance.

---

11. Evaluate Results, Not Just Effort

Effort is appreciated—but leadership requires results.

After completion, ask:

- Did they achieve the objective?
- What went well?
- What needs improvement?
- What support do they need next time?

Evaluation strengthens their skill and your leadership.

---

12. Delegation Expands Your Leadership Capacity

When you delegate effectively, you gain:

- More time
- More clarity
- More strategic thinking
- More innovation
- More organizational strength
- More leadership presence

You are able to focus on what truly matters:

Vision. Direction. Strategy. Growth.

Delegation transforms you from a worker into a leader—

a leader who builds systems, empowers people, and drives long-term success.

Delegation is not just a leadership skill—it is a leadership requirement.

You cannot reach your highest level alone.

You need people you trust, people you develop, and people you empower.

When you delegate with strength and respect, your team becomes unstoppable.

CHAPTER 29 — Conflict Management: Staying Strong in Tension

When handled well, conflict can:

- Strengthen relationships
- Build mutual respect
- Clarify expectations
- Improve communication
- Fix broken processes
- Reveal deeper issues
- Increase trust

Conflict is not the enemy—emotional reactions are.

Handled with maturity, conflict becomes a powerful leadership tool.

---

14. Never Avoid Necessary Conflict

Avoiding conflict doesn't protect relationships—it slowly destroys them.

Avoidance leads to:

- Hidden resentment
- Repeated problems
- Unclear expectations
- Declining performance
- Weak leadership presence

Strong leaders address issues early before they grow into crises.

Facing conflict builds trust.

Avoiding conflict weakens leadership.

---

15. Choose the Right Environment for Tough Conversations

Timing and environment matter.

Never address conflict when:

- You're angry
- The other person is emotional
- The environment is public
- The moment is rushed

Instead, choose:

- Privacy
- Neutral location
- Calm timing
- A focused mindset

Leaders control the setting to control the outcome.

---

16. Use "I" Statements Instead of "You" Attacks

This shifts the tone from accusation to clarity.

Instead of:

"You're not doing your job."

Say:

"I need these tasks completed on time, and here's why it matters."

"I" statements prevent defensiveness and promote understanding.

---

17. Keep the Goal in Front

The purpose of conflict management is **resolution**, not winning.

Leaders focus on:

- Alignment
- Improvement
- Future performance
- Solutions
- Professional respect

The goal is progress—not victory.

---

18. Remain Objective, Not Emotional

Objectivity gives you control.

Objectivity means focusing on:

- Facts
- Behavior
- Standards
- Outcomes

Not:

- Personal feelings
- Past frustrations
- Bias
- Ego

Objectivity strengthens your credibility.

---

19. Know When to Escalate Professionally

If someone refuses accountability or continues breaking standards, leaders must escalate.

Escalation may include:

- Additional coaching
- Written expectations
- Formal warnings
- Reassigning responsibilities
- In serious cases, removal

Escalation is not punishment—it protects the mission and the team.

---

20. End Conflict With Clear Agreements

Every conflict conversation should end with clarity.

Both sides must know:

- What was discussed
- What needs to change
- What the expectations are
- What the next steps will be
- What support is available
- What the consequences will be if it happens again

Clarity removes room for misinterpretation.

---

21. Document Important Conversations

Professional leaders keep records of major conflict resolutions to protect:

- Themselves
- The mission
- The organization
- The individual involved

Documentation ensures consistency and transparency.

---

22. Follow Up to Ensure Progress

Conflict is not resolved when the conversation ends—

it's resolved when the behavior changes.

Follow-up shows:

- Leadership engagement
- Accountability
- Commitment to improvement
- Support for growth

Leaders don't hope for improvement—they verify it.

---

23. Conflict Makes You a Stronger, More Respected Leader

When you manage conflict well, people begin to see you as:

- Resilient

- Emotionally intelligent
- Fair
- Consistent
- Reliable
- Strong
- Trustworthy

People respect leaders who stay steady under tension.

---

24. Conflict Is a Leadership Skill—Master It

Mastering conflict will help you:

- Build stronger teams
- Create clearer expectations
- Maintain higher standards
- Strengthen communication
- Protect the mission
- Increase respect
- Build confidence in your presence

The ability to remain calm, direct, and solution-focused during conflict is one of the greatest advantages a leader can possess.

Leaders who handle conflict well never lose control—they guide it, shape it, and resolve it with strength and clarity.

Conflict doesn't break great leaders—

it reveals them.

CHAPTER 30 — Building a Culture of Discipline and Accountability

Great organizations, strong teams, and transformational leaders all have one thing in common:

a culture built on discipline and accountability.

Discipline creates consistency.

Accountability ensures responsibility.

Together, they create environments where excellence becomes the norm—not the exception.

Most people talk about success, but very few build the habits required to sustain it. CEOs understand that culture is not created by chance—it is created by design. It is built through standards, systems, behavior, and leadership. A disciplined culture multiplies performance. A culture without accountability collapses.

When you create a culture of discipline and accountability, you create a team—and a life—that moves with purpose, consistency, and strength.

---

1. Culture Begins With the Leader

People rise—or fall—to the level of leadership.

A leader sets the tone by:

- Maintaining high personal standards
- Showing up consistently
- Demonstrating professionalism
- Following through on commitments
- Being accountable themselves

If the leader is sloppy, the culture becomes sloppy.

If the leader is disciplined, the culture becomes disciplined.

---

2. Discipline Is the Foundation of High Performance

Discipline is doing what needs to be done—

even when you don't feel like doing it.

A disciplined culture includes:

- Clear routines
- Organized processes
- Consistent behavior
- Daily execution
- A focus on results

Discipline creates predictability and reliability.

---

3. Accountability Creates Ownership

Accountability is not punishment.

It is responsibility.

A culture of accountability means:

- Everyone knows their role
- Everyone owns their performance
- No one hides mistakes
- No one blames others
- Everyone contributes to the mission

Accountability creates maturity and growth.

---

4. Set Clear Standards That Everyone Understands

You cannot enforce what you do not define.

Standards should be:

- Written
- Communicated
- Measurable
- Visible
- Non-negotiable

When standards are unclear, people guess.

When standards are clear, people perform.

---

5. Make Expectations Simple and Direct

Discipline thrives on clarity, not confusion.

Strong leaders communicate expectations:

- Directly
- Professionally
- Without emotional tone
- Without vague language
- With clear deadlines

Clarity eliminates excuses.

---

6. Build Systems That Support Discipline

People don't rise to the level of motivation—they rise to the level of systems.

Systems include:

- Processes
- Checklists
- Structures
- Routines
- Accountability checkpoints

Systems make discipline easy and automatic.

---

7. Hold People Accountable with Professionalism

Accountability must be consistent.

Leaders enforce accountability by:

- Addressing issues immediately
- Correcting behavior, not attacking character
- Explaining consequences
- Following through when necessary

- Providing support for improvement

Consistency builds respect.

---

8. Praise Discipline as Much as You Correct Mistakes

People repeat what gets recognized.

Celebrate:

- Consistency
- Improvement
- Follow-through
- High standards
- Reliability

Recognition fuels discipline.

---

9. Address Violations Without Delay

Ignoring small issues creates big problems.

A delayed response leads to:

- Lower standards
- Poor performance
- Disrespect
- Loss of trust
- Cultural breakdown

Correcting issues early keeps culture strong.

---

10. Create a Safe Environment for Ownership

People will only accept responsibility when they feel safe to be honest.

Build trust by:

- Listening without judgment
- Encouraging honesty
- Treating mistakes as learning opportunities
- Supporting development

- Allowing transparency

When people feel safe, they take ownership instead of hiding.

---

11. Enforce Standards Fairly and Equally

Nothing destroys culture faster than favoritism.

Leaders must:

- Hold everyone to the same rules
- Enforce expectations consistently
- Avoid double standards
- Keep personal feelings out of decisions

Fairness builds trust and respect.

---

12. Build a Culture Where Excuses Don't Exist

Excuses are the enemy of discipline.

A strong culture replaces excuses with:

- Solutions
- Adjustment
- Ownership
- Professionalism

Leaders do not entertain excuses—they redirect to responsibility.

---

13. Teach People to Self-Correct

True accountability is not enforced from the outside—it is developed inside.

Help your team learn to self-correct by teaching them to ask:

- "What went wrong?"
- "What can I do better?"
- "What will I improve next time?"

Self-correction builds leaders, not followers.

---

14. Discipline Creates Freedom

Most people think discipline restricts them.

In reality, discipline creates freedom.

Discipline gives you:

- Freedom from chaos
- Freedom from inconsistency
- Freedom from stress
- Freedom from confusion
- Freedom to perform at higher levels

Discipline is a form of self-respect.

---

15. Accountability Strengthens Trust

People trust leaders who:

- Keep their word
- Maintain integrity
- Enforce fairness
- Communicate clearly
- Take responsibility

Trust grows in environments where accountability is the norm.

---

16. Culture Must Be Reinforced Daily

Culture is not built once—it is maintained daily.

Leaders reinforce culture by:

- Leading by example
- Keeping standards visible
- Maintaining consistent routines
- Addressing issues immediately
- Recognizing excellence consistently

Culture is the daily behavior of the environment.

A disciplined, accountable culture doesn't happen by accident—it is created intentionally by leaders who refuse to lower their standards.

When you build this culture, you create a team—and a life—that is unstoppable.

People perform better.

Systems run smoother.

Results increase.

Leadership becomes easier.

Discipline creates stability.

Accountability creates excellence.

Together, they create greatness.

- "I can handle this."
- "This won't break me."
- "I'll find a way."
- "This challenge is shaping me."
- "I don't quit when it's hard—I grow through it."

Your mindset determines your ability to withstand adversity.

---

2. Resilient Leaders Accept Reality Instead of Resisting It

Resistance creates stress.

Acceptance creates control.

When something goes wrong, resilient leaders don't waste time complaining or denying. They acknowledge the situation quickly and shift into solution mode.

Acceptance is not surrender—it is awareness.

Awareness gives you power.

CHAPTER 31 — Thinking Like an Owner, Not an Employee

There is a clear difference between people who stay stuck and people who rise to leadership:

owners think differently than employees.

Even if you don't own the company you work for, adopting an ownership mindset transforms your success, your confidence, and your opportunities. CEOs rise because they think like owners. They take responsibility. They anticipate needs. They solve problems without being told. They treat the mission as if it were their own.

Employees wait to be led.

Owners rise to lead.

This mindset shift is powerful—it changes how you work, how you show up, and how people perceive your value.

---

1. Owners Take Responsibility—Employees Avoid It

Employees say:

"That's not my job."

"I wasn't told to do that."

Owners say:

"I'll handle it."

"I'll figure it out."

"How can we improve this?"

Responsibility is the foundation of leadership.

When you take ownership, you become indispensable.

---

2. Owners See the Big Picture

Employees focus on their single task.

Owners focus on the mission.

Owners ask:

- "How does this decision affect the whole system?"
- "How will this benefit the long-term goal?"
- "What's the ripple effect of this change?"

Thinking big strengthens your leadership presence.

---

3. Owners Solve Problems—Employees Point Them Out

Employees bring problems.

Owners bring solutions.

Instead of saying, "This is broken," owners say:

"Here's the issue—and here's my suggested fix."

Every problem you solve increases your value.

Solutions build leadership credibility.

---

4. Owners Don't Wait for Permission

Employees wait to be told.

Owners take initiative.

Initiative looks like:

- Starting tasks early
- Preparing ahead of time
- Offering help before being asked
- Seeing what needs to be done and doing it

Initiative makes you stand out instantly.

---

5. Owners Manage Time Like a Leader

Employees clock in and clock out.

Owners measure their work by impact.

Owners don't waste time on:

- Distractions

- Gossip
- Complaining
- Low-value tasks

They focus on what moves the mission forward.

---

6. Owners Protect the Brand and Reputation

Owners treat the organization as an extension of themselves.

They care about:

- Customer experience
- Company image
- Team morale
- Quality
- Professionalism

Their pride elevates the entire environment.

---

7. Owners Focus on Results, Not Excuses

Employees explain why something didn't get done.

Owners focus on making sure it gets done.

Results matter more than explanations.

When you think like an owner, excuses disappear.

---

8. Owners Take Accountability Without Defensiveness

Employees get defensive.

Owners get responsible.

Accountability sounds like:

"I understand the issue. I'll correct it."

"Here's the plan to fix it moving forward."

This maturity is what earns trust and leadership opportunities.

---

9. Owners Respect Resources

Employees waste resources because they don't see the impact.

Owners maximize resources because they think long-term.

Owners care about:

- Time
- Money
- Equipment
- Information
- People

They use resources wisely because they see the connection to the mission.

---

10. Owners Anticipate Needs Before They Arise

Employees react.

Owners predict.

Ownership thinking includes:

- Foreseeing potential problems
- Preparing solutions in advance
- Planning for tomorrow, not just today

This anticipation makes you a strategic leader.

---

11. Owners Communicate Like Leaders

Owners communicate with clarity, confidence, and professionalism.

Their communication is:

- Direct
- Respectful
- Timely
- Solution-focused
- Aligned with the mission

Strong communication increases your influence.

---

12. Owners Never Say "That's Not My Problem"

That sentence destroys careers.

People who climb take ownership, not distance.

Owners understand that every success—and every failure—affects the entire team.

---

13. Owners Embrace Continuous Learning

Employees stay comfortable.

Owners improve constantly.

They read.

They study.

They ask questions.

They seek feedback.

They learn new skills.

Growth is part of their identity.

---

14. Owners Build Relationships, Not Divisions

Owners understand that success requires teamwork.

They:

- Build trust
- Resolve conflicts
- Support others
- Communicate clearly
- Protect unity

Strong relationships create strong organizations.

---

15. Owners Think in Terms of Opportunity, Not Obstacles

Employees see problems.

Owners see possibilities.

Owners ask:

"What opportunity is hidden inside this situation?"

"How can this challenge make us better?"

This mindset creates resilience and innovation.

---

16. Owners Keep Standards High Even Without Supervision

Employees do well when watched.

Owners do well because it's who they are.

Integrity is demonstrated when no one is watching.

---

17. Owners Don't Take Shortcuts

Shortcuts weaken trust.

Owners do things the right way, not the easy way.

Quality builds reputation.

Reputation builds influence.

---

18. Owners Rise Into Leadership Naturally

When you think like an owner:

- Leaders notice you
- Responsibilities increase
- Opportunities find you
- People trust you
- Your presence grows
- Your value multiplies

Ownership makes you a leader long before the title ever arrives.

Thinking like an owner transforms your mindset, your discipline, your influence, and your future.

It elevates you above average.

It sets you apart as a leader.

It positions you for success at the highest level.

The moment you stop thinking like an employee and start thinking like an owner, your entire life rises.

CHAPTER 32 — Building Resilience and Mental Toughness

(Expanded Version)

Resilience and mental toughness are the backbone of leadership. Every CEO, every high performer, every world-class leader has one thing in common: they refuse to break when life applies pressure. They may bend, but they never break. They experience setbacks, but they always bounce back. They face challenges, but they rise above them with strength and clarity.

Mental toughness is not about being emotionless—it's about being **unshakeable**.

Resilience is not about avoiding struggle—it's about mastering it.

Greatness is built through resistance.

Resilience is built through experience.

Strength is built through surviving what was meant to stop you.

The more resilient you become, the further you rise.

---

1. Mental Toughness Begins With Your Mindset

Your thoughts shape your resilience.

When pressure hits, your inner voice becomes your greatest weapon—or your greatest enemy.

Mentally tough people think:

- "I can handle this."
- "This won't break me."
- "I'll find a way."
- "This challenge is shaping me."
- "I don't quit when it's hard—I grow through it."

Your mindset determines your ability to withstand adversity.

---

2. Resilient Leaders Accept Reality Instead of Resisting It

Resistance creates stress.

Acceptance creates control.

When something goes wrong, resilient leaders don't waste time complaining or denying. They acknowledge the situation quickly and shift into solution mode.

Acceptance is not surrender—it is awareness.

Awareness gives you power.

---

3. Pressure Is an Opportunity for Growth

Most people avoid pressure.

High performers embrace it.

Pressure helps you:

- Sharpen your skills
- Strengthen your character
- Reveal your weaknesses
- Build emotional endurance
- Grow your confidence

Pressure is not your enemy—it is your training.

---

4. Resilience Requires Emotional Control

You cannot be mentally tough if your emotions control you.

Tough leaders:

- Stay calm under stress
- Think clearly when others panic
- Pause before reacting
- Keep their tone steady
- Respond with logic, not emotion

Emotional control is the superpower of resilience.

---

5. Every Challenge Becomes a Lesson

Mentally tough people convert adversity into wisdom.

After each challenge, they ask:

- "What did this teach me?"
- "How can I grow from this?"
- "What skill did this develop?"
- "What mistake will I never repeat?"

Challenges don't weaken them—they upgrade them.

---

6. Build a Higher "Stress Threshold"

Your ability to handle stress increases as you expose yourself to it in controlled ways.

You build toughness by:

- Taking on difficult tasks
- Finishing commitments even when tired
- Doing uncomfortable things
- Practicing self-discipline daily
- Facing problems directly

The more pressure you survive, the stronger you become.

---

7. Stay Focused When Life Gets Hard

Distractions increase under stress.

Mentally tough people narrow their focus.

They ask:

- "What matters right now?"
- "What can I control?"
- "What is my next best move?"

Focus continues progress when situations feel overwhelming.

---

8. Surround Yourself With Strength

Your environment influences your resilience.

You weaken when you surround yourself with:

- Complainers
- Quitters
- Negative thinkers
- People who avoid responsibility
- People who crumble under pressure

You grow when you surround yourself with:

- Leaders
- Thinkers
- Problem-solvers
- High achievers
- People who challenge you

Strong environments build strong minds.

---

9. Build Internal Confidence Through Action

Confidence doesn't come from motivation—it comes from evidence.

You build confidence when you:

- Keep your promises to yourself
- Follow your routines
- Stay disciplined
- Overcome challenges
- Do the hard things you don't feel like doing

Each victory increases your inner strength.

---

10. Resilient Leaders Adapt, Not Break

Life doesn't always go as planned.

Resilient leaders pivot instead of panic.

They adjust their:

- Strategy
- Expectations
- Timeline
- Approach

Adaptation is proof of strength, not weakness.

---

11. Mental Toughness Requires Energy Management

You cannot stay strong if your battery is empty.

High performers protect their energy by:

- Resting strategically
- Eating well
- Exercising consistently
- Sleeping properly
- Limiting draining people
- Managing stress intentionally

Energy fuels resilience.

---

12. Stay Grounded in Your Purpose

Purpose is your resilience anchor.

When you know why you are fighting, you can survive any challenge.

Purpose makes obstacles smaller.

Purpose makes pain meaningful.

Purpose gives you the strength to persist.

---

13. Failure Is Not the End—It Is Information

Failure only breaks those who see it as final.

Resilient leaders see failure as:

- Feedback
- Direction
- A new strategy opportunity

- A temporary disruption
- A stepping stone

They refuse to let failure define them.

---

14. Choose Strength Every Day

Resilience is a daily decision.

It's built through consistent habits—not one-time moments.

Every day you:

- Wake up with intention
- Do hard things
- Stay disciplined
- Control your reactions
- Keep moving forward

—you build mental toughness.

Resilience and mental toughness turn ordinary people into extraordinary leaders.

They give you the ability to stay unshakeable in chaos, powerful under pressure, and consistent through difficulty.

The stronger you become internally, the more unstoppable you become externally.

Resilience is not a gift—

it is a choice, a practice, and a commitment to your own strength.

CHAPTER 33 — Leading Through Change and Transition

Change is one of the most difficult realities of leadership.

People don't resist change itself—they resist the *uncertainty* that comes with it. They resist the fear of the unknown, the loss of comfort, and the disruption of routines. A true leader understands this deeply and knows how to guide people through transition with confidence, clarity, and stability.

Change is inevitable.

Growth is optional.

Leadership determines which direction people choose.

To lead effectively through change, you must be stronger, clearer, and more grounded than the environment around you.

---

1. Change Requires Strong Leadership, Not Loud Leadership

During transition, people look for stability.

They pay attention to your tone, your decisions, your body language, and your confidence.

Strong leaders:

- Stay calm
- Stay objective
- Communicate clearly
- Avoid panic
- Set the emotional tone

If the leader is steady, the team stays steady.

---

2. Accept Change Before You Lead Others Through It

You cannot guide people through something you haven't accepted yourself.

Leaders embrace change by saying:

- "This is happening."
- "Let's move forward with a plan."
- "Here's how we can use this to our advantage."

Acceptance gives you clarity.

Clarity gives you authority.

---

3. Communicate Early, Clearly, and Frequently

Silence creates fear.

Clarity creates confidence.

When leading through transition, effective communication must include:

- What is changing
- Why it's happening
- How it affects everyone
- What the plan is
- What support is available
- What the next steps are

People fear what they don't understand.

Your job is to bring understanding.

---

4. Provide Certainty Wherever Possible

Even when the situation is uncertain, leaders provide certainty in:

- Expectations
- Roles
- Standards
- Values
- Strategy
- Communication

People can handle change when they still feel grounded in something stable.

---

5. Address the Emotional Side of Change

Change triggers emotions—fear, frustration, worry, confusion.

Strong leaders don't ignore emotions. They acknowledge them and redirect the focus toward solutions.

A leader might say:

"I understand this feels sudden. Let's talk about how we can navigate this together."

Emotional intelligence builds trust.

---

6. Focus on Solutions, Not the Disruption

When change happens, most people focus on:

- What went wrong
- What they lost
- What they fear

Leaders focus on:

- What opportunities exist
- What can be improved
- What new strengths can be developed
- What the next step is

Your focus determines the team's energy.

---

7. Create a Transition Plan, Not Chaos

A clear transition plan answers:

- What is changing?
- When is it changing?
- Who is affected?
- What steps must be taken?

- What resources are needed?
- Who is responsible?

Structure turns confusion into organization.

---

8. Empower People During the Process

People feel powerless during change.

Give them roles and responsibilities that help them feel in control.

Empowerment increases:

- Confidence
- Engagement
- Participation
- Commitment
- Ownership

When people feel part of the solution, resistance decreases.

---

9. Be Visible and Accessible

During transition, leaders cannot disappear.

Be present.

Be available.

Be engaged.

Visibility builds trust.

Silence builds fear.

---

10. Address Resistance With Understanding, Not Force

Resistance is normal.

People resist because they fear losing something.

Strong leaders:

- Listen
- Ask questions
- Understand concerns

- Provide clarity
- Show benefits
- Set expectations

You cannot eliminate resistance, but you can minimize it through leadership.

---

11. Reinforce the "Why" Behind the Change

People accept change faster when the reason is clear.

Explain:

- The long-term benefits
- The mission behind the shift
- The opportunities created
- The problems being solved

Purpose reduces fear.

---

12. Protect Morale During Transition

Change can weaken morale if not managed well.

Leaders protect morale by:

- Celebrating progress
- Recognizing effort
- Keeping communication positive
- Correcting misinformation
- Encouraging unity

High morale accelerates transition.

---

13. Be Flexible, But Stay Firm on the Mission

Flexibility helps people adapt.

Firmness keeps everyone aligned.

Leaders adjust the *approach*, not the *mission*.

---

14. Lead With Confidence, Even When You Don't Have Every Answer

A leader doesn't need all the answers—

they need to show that a path forward exists.

People follow confidence, not perfection.

They follow direction, not certainty.

---

15. Monitor Progress and Adjust When Necessary

Change is not a one-time event—

it is a process.

Leaders monitor:

- Team performance
- Emotional climate
- Effectiveness of new systems
- Areas of confusion
- Unexpected challenges

Flexibility ensures success.

---

16. Celebrate Milestones

Celebrations reinforce progress and encourage perseverance.

Recognize:

- Adaptation
- Improvement
- Teamwork
- Achievement
- Resilience

Recognition strengthens motivation and unity.

---

17. Reflect and Learn After the Transition

Every transition leaves lessons behind.

Leaders reflect on:

- What went well
- What could improve
- What was learned
- What systems need reinforcement
- What communication worked best

Reflection strengthens future leadership.

Change is not the enemy of progress—

it is the engine of progress.

Leaders who can guide people through uncertainty become irreplaceable.

They build trust.

They build stability.

They build momentum.

They build stronger teams and stronger futures.

Your ability to lead through transition determines the strength of your leadership.

When you stay steady, the people you lead become steady.

When you stay confident, they become confident.

When you lead with clarity, they move with purpose.

That is the power of a true leader.

CHAPTER 34 — The Discipline of Long-Term Vision

Long-term vision is the compass that directs every great leader. It is the ability to see further than today, think beyond the moment, and make decisions that will matter years from now. While most people live in the urgency of the present, CEOs build from the perspective of the future. They don't just react—they *design* their life, their success, and their legacy.

Vision gives your life direction.

Discipline keeps you on that direction.

A long-term vision transforms your choices, your habits, your environment, and your priorities. It turns you from a participant in life to a creator of your destiny.

---

1. Vision Begins with Understanding Your Ultimate Destination

You cannot build a future you cannot see.

Your long-term vision must be clear enough to inspire you and strong enough to pull you forward.

Ask yourself:

- "Where do I want to be in five years?"
- "What kind of leader do I want to become?"
- "What lifestyle am I building?"
- "What legacy am I leaving?"

Vision is not a dream—

it is a direction.

---

2. A Strong Vision Requires Discipline Every Single Day

Vision without discipline is imagination.

Discipline without vision is wasted effort.

Leaders maintain their long-term vision by:

- Sticking to routines
- Practicing self-control
- Prioritizing high-value tasks
- Making sacrifices
- Staying consistent even when motivation is low

Success is built through disciplined daily actions that align with your vision.

---

3. Vision Helps You Make Better Decisions

When you have a long-term vision, decision-making becomes easier.

You simply ask:

"Does this align with my future or distract from it?"

If the answer is no, the decision is made.

Vision removes confusion and eliminates distractions.

---

4. Vision Gives You Strength During Hard Times

The stronger the vision, the stronger the leader.

When challenges hit, vision reminds you why you must keep going.

It gives you endurance when you feel tired, discipline when you feel distracted, and courage when you feel uncertain.

Vision is the anchor that holds you steady during storms.

---

5. Most People Fail Because They Think Too Short-Term

Short-term thinking causes people to:

- Quit too early
- Fear temporary discomfort
- Seek instant gratification
- Avoid long-term investments
- Lose focus when results aren't immediate

Leaders operate with patience and foresight.

They understand that consistency beats intensity.

---

6. A Long-Term Vision Requires You to Delay Pleasure

Great leaders make sacrifices today to enjoy freedoms tomorrow.

They give up:

- Unnecessary spending
- Excessive entertainment
- Negative environments
- Toxic habits
- Short-term comfort

So they can build:

- Financial freedom
- Strong leadership
- Powerful opportunities
- Lasting success

Delaying gratification is a discipline of the elite.

---

7. Vision Expands Your Thinking

Your vision determines how big you think.

Small goals produce small effort.

Big goals produce growth, strategy, and high-level thinking.

Long-term vision forces you to:

- Plan differently
- Work differently
- Think differently
- Lead differently

Big vision expands your potential.

---

8. Long-Term Vision Creates Leadership Confidence

When you know where you're going, you walk differently.

You speak differently.

You operate with purpose.

Confidence comes from clarity.

Clarity comes from vision.

People follow leaders who know their direction.

---

9. Vision Requires You to Protect Your Environment

Your environment must support your future, not sabotage it.

To protect your vision, you must guard against:

- Negative people
- Draining relationships
- Unproductive habits
- Distractions
- Environments without growth

Your vision will not survive in a toxic environment.

---

10. Vision Requires Strategic Planning

Long-term leaders don't leave their future to chance.

They create a plan.

A strategic vision includes:

- A clear destination
- Measurable milestones
- Daily disciplines
- Monthly adjustments
- Annual goals

Planning strengthens direction.

---

11. Long-Term Vision Forces Growth

Your current level of thinking, discipline, and habits will not take you where you want to go.

Your future demands a stronger, sharper version of you.

Vision stretches you.

It pushes you.

It forces you to evolve into the person capable of achieving it.

Growth is the natural result of pursuing something bigger than yourself.

---

12. Vision Must Be Reviewed Regularly

Life changes.

Goals evolve.

Situations shift.

Smart leaders revisit their vision often to ensure alignment and clarity.

They adjust the strategy—not the destination.

Reviewing your vision keeps your focus sharp.

---

13. Vision Creates Legacy

A long-term vision is not just about success today—it's about impact tomorrow.

Legacy includes:

- What you build
- Who you help
- How you lead
- What you leave behind
- Who you become

Legacy is created through decades of consistent, disciplined, visionary leadership.

Vision is not a moment—it is a mission.

It guides your steps, sharpens your actions, strengthens your discipline, and defines your future.

When you learn to think long-term, live with purpose, and operate with daily discipline, you step into the mindset of a CEO—the mindset that creates power, opportunity, and lasting success.

Your long-term vision is your blueprint.

Your discipline is the construction.

Your future is the result.

CHAPTER 35 — The Mindset of Innovation and Creativity

Innovation is the lifeblood of leadership.

Creativity is the spark that ignites new ideas, new solutions, and new opportunities. CEOs understand that success is not built by repeating the past—it's built by imagining the future. The greatest leaders are innovators, thinkers, and problem-solvers who see possibilities where others see limitations.

Innovation is not limited to technology or inventions.

It's a mindset—a way of thinking that challenges the ordinary and demands improvement.

Creativity is not artistic talent—it's the ability to see connections, discover new angles, and think beyond what already exists.

To rise as a leader, you must learn to think differently, act differently, and question everything that limits progress.

---

1. Innovation Starts With Curiosity

Curiosity opens the mind.

Without it, creativity dies.

Innovative leaders are always asking:

- "What if…?"
- "Why not?"
- "How can we make this better?"
- "What is the opportunity inside this problem?"

Curiosity turns ordinary thinkers into visionary leaders.

---

2. Creativity Requires an Open Mind

You cannot innovate with a closed mindset.

Creative leaders remain open to:

- New ideas
- Different perspectives
- Unfamiliar strategies
- Constructive criticism
- Alternative methods

Being open-minded does not mean accepting everything—it means being willing to explore new possibilities.

---

3. Innovation Comes From Challenging the Status Quo

Average people protect the old way.

Leaders challenge it.

They ask:

"Is there a more efficient way?"

"Is this system outdated?"

"Is there a better process we haven't tried yet?"

Innovation requires courage to question what everyone else accepts.

---

4. Creativity Thrives in Environments of Freedom

You cannot innovate if you are afraid of being wrong.

Leaders build environments where people feel safe to:

- Experiment
- Share ideas
- Test strategies
- Think differently
- Fail without punishment

Freedom fuels creativity.

---

5. Innovation Requires Taking Calculated Risks

No progress is made without risk.

Innovative leaders understand that every breakthrough includes:

- Uncertainty
- Trial and error
- Learning
- Adjustment

They don't fear risk—they manage it.

Risk is the bridge between ideas and results.

---

6. Creativity Is Connecting What Others Don't See

Creativity is not always about creating something new—it's often about connecting old ideas in new ways.

Creative leaders combine:

- Concepts
- Tools
- Strategies
- Perspectives

Innovation is often hidden in the intersection of ideas.

---

7. Innovation Solves Problems, Not Creates Them

The purpose of innovation is improvement.

Innovative leaders solve problems by asking:

- "What is the true issue here?"
- "What solution will have the greatest impact?"
- "How can we simplify this?"
- "How can we make this more efficient?"

Innovation makes things easier, faster, better, or more effective.

---

8. Creativity Requires Breaking Mental Limits

Your mind must be free before your ideas can be.

Innovative leaders break mental barriers by:

- Allowing themselves to think big

- Challenging fear-based thoughts
- Refusing self-doubt
- Seeing possibilities instead of restrictions

Your thinking creates your limits—or destroys them.

---

9. Innovation Requires Continuous Learning

The more you know, the more ideas you can generate.

Innovative leaders:

- Study things outside their industry
- Read constantly
- Learn new skills
- Stay curious about emerging technologies
- Expand their knowledge

A growing mind produces fresh ideas.

---

10. Creativity Requires Time, Space, and Reflection

In the chaos of life, creativity gets buried.

Leaders protect creative time by:

- Scheduling thinking time
- Taking breaks to recharge
- Disconnecting from distractions
- Creating quiet environments
- Allowing space for reflection

Creativity needs room to breathe.

---

11. Innovation Requires Execution

Ideas mean nothing without action.

Innovative leaders understand:

- Ideas start the movement
- Action makes it real

- Consistency makes it successful
- Discipline makes it sustainable

Creativity without execution is just imagination.

---

12. Creativity Thrives in Collaboration

Innovation grows when multiple minds come together.

Leaders encourage collaboration because it:

- Expands thinking
- Combines strengths
- Uncovers blind spots
- Sparks new ideas
- Improves solution quality

Great ideas rarely come from isolation—they come from connection.

---

13. Innovation Requires Resilience

Not every idea succeeds.

Not every attempt works.

Innovative leaders:

- Adjust
- Test again
- Improve
- Learn
- Persist

Failure is not the opposite of innovation—it is part of the process.

---

14. Creativity Inspires Others

When you think creatively, you give others permission to do the same.

Creative leaders:

- Raise team morale
- Build excitement

- Spark innovation in others
- Create an environment of growth
- Inspire new breakthroughs

Creativity is contagious.

---

15. Innovation Separates Leaders From Followers

Leaders innovate.

Followers repeat.

Innovation gives you:

- Influence
- Authority
- Competitive advantage
- Strategic leverage
- Long-term relevance

Innovation keeps you valuable in any industry.

Innovation and creativity are not talents—they are habits.

They grow with practice.

They strengthen with courage.

They expand with curiosity.

They flourish with discipline.

When you learn to think like an innovator, you transform into a leader who is not limited by the present, but inspired by the future.

Your creativity is your advantage.

Your innovation is your power.

Your ideas are your leadership currency.

Use them boldly.

CHAPTER 36 — Mastering High-Level Communication Skills

Communication is one of the most powerful skills a leader can possess. It shapes relationships, influences decisions, resolves conflicts, inspires action, and sets the tone for your entire organization or environment. CEOs do not simply *talk*—they communicate with strategy, clarity, and intention.

High-level communication is not about being loud, dominant, or impressive.

It's about being **effective**.

It's knowing how to deliver the right message, at the right time, in the right tone, to achieve the right outcome.

Great leaders speak with purpose.

They listen with discipline.

They respond with clarity.

They communicate to win hearts, minds, and results.

Communication is not a soft skill—

it is a leadership weapon.

---

1. Great Leaders Communicate With Clarity

Clarity eliminates confusion.

Confusion destroys progress.

High-level communicators use:

- Direct language
- Simple words
- Clear expectations
- Structured messages

No guessing.

No vague phrasing.

No mixed signals.

When you speak clearly, people follow confidently.

---

2. Listening Is More Important Than Speaking

Most people listen to respond.

Leaders listen to understand.

High-level listening means:

- Being fully present
- Paying attention to tone and body language
- Asking clarifying questions
- Avoiding interruptions
- Listening to the meaning behind the words

When people feel heard, they respect your leadership more.

---

3. Control Your Tone—It Carries More Weight Than Words

A message can be correct, but the wrong tone can destroy it.

Tone communicates:

- Confidence
- Respect
- Authority
- Calmness
- Professionalism

Leaders maintain a steady tone, even in conflict or pressure.

Your tone shows your emotional discipline.

---

4. Communicate With Purpose, Not Emotion

Effective communication is strategic, not reactive.

High-level communicators think before they speak.

They ask themselves:

- "What outcome do I want?"

- "What is the best way to say this?"
- "How will this message be received?"
- "Is this emotion or logic speaking?"

Purposeful communication protects relationships and increases influence.

---

5. Use Brevity—Say More With Less

Long speeches lose attention.

Powerful leaders get to the point.

Brevity is the ability to communicate:

- Clearly
- Directly
- Briefly
- Efficiently

People trust leaders who don't waste time with unnecessary words.

---

6. Nonverbal Communication Shapes Everything

Your body speaks before your mouth opens.

Nonverbal signals include:

- Eye contact
- Posture
- Facial expression
- Hand movement
- Energy
- Confidence

High-level communication requires body language that matches your message.

---

7. Ask High-Quality Questions

Great communicators don't just give answers—they ask questions that:

- Reveal information
- Clarify perspectives
- Solve problems
- Guide decisions
- Build trust

Good questions create great leadership.

---

8. Adapt Your Communication to Your Audience

One message does not fit all.

High-level leaders adjust their approach based on:

- Personality
- Experience
- Culture
- Emotional state
- Communication style
- Authority level

Flexibility increases impact.

---

9. Communicate Expectations Without Apology

Leaders cannot afford hesitation.

Expectations should be delivered with:

- Confidence
- Directness
- Professional tone
- Clarity
- Firmness

People rise to clear expectations.

---

10. Master the Art of Professionalism

Professional communication means:

- No gossip

- No emotional outbursts
- No disrespect
- No sarcasm
- No passive-aggressive comments

Professionalism strengthens credibility.

---

11. Use Feedback as a Leadership Tool

Feedback is how leaders shape performance.

Effective feedback is:

- Clear
- Specific
- Respectful
- Behavior-focused
- Solution-oriented

High-level leaders correct without humiliating.

---

12. Handle Difficult Conversations With Strength

Leaders cannot avoid uncomfortable conversations.

To handle them well:

- Stay calm
- Speak directly
- Use facts, not emotion
- Maintain respect
- Keep the goal in front
- End with clear next steps

Difficult conversations build strong cultures.

---

13. Inspire Through Communication

Leadership is influence—

and influence is communication.

Inspirational communication includes:

- Vision
- Confidence
- Emotion delivered with control
- Stories that resonate
- Words that motivate action

Leaders inspire people to believe in something bigger.

---

14. Communication Must Match Your Integrity

People listen to your words, but they follow your actions.

If your communication is strong but your actions are weak, your leadership collapses.

High-level communication requires consistency between:

- What you say
- What you do
- What you stand for

Integrity is the foundation of influence.

---

15. Leaders Communicate to Build, Not Destroy

Your communication should elevate:

- Trust
- Understanding
- Direction
- Unity
- Purpose
- Momentum

Wise leaders use communication to strengthen environments, not weaken them.

High-level communication transforms you into a powerful leader.

It makes you more influential, more respected, and more effective in every environment.

When you learn to communicate with clarity, discipline, confidence, and emotional intelligence,

you speak like a CEO.

You lead like a CEO.

And you rise like a CEO.

Communication is not just a skill—

it is the language of leadership.

CHAPTER 37 — Building a High-Performance Team

A high-performance team is the engine behind every successful leader, organization, and mission. No matter how talented you are, your results will always be limited if the people around you cannot execute, collaborate, or stay aligned with the vision. CEOs understand that their true power lies not in doing everything themselves, but in building a strong, disciplined, and high-performing team around them.

A high-performance team does not happen by accident.

It is built intentionally through leadership, clarity, culture, and accountability.

When you build the right team, success becomes a collective force—not a solo effort.

---

1. Great Teams Start With Great Leadership

The team can only rise to the level of the leader.

A strong leader sets the foundation by:

- Demonstrating discipline
- Providing clarity
- Offering support
- Setting direction
- Modeling the standards

The leader is the thermostat—the team's performance rises or falls based on your example.

---

2. Define the Mission Clearly

People perform better when they understand the purpose behind their work.

High-performance teams know:

- Why the mission matters
- What the goals are
- What success looks like
- How each person contributes

Clarity creates alignment.

Alignment creates momentum.

---

3. Hire and Build Around Strengths

You don't build a high-performance team by filling seats—you build it by filling roles with people whose strengths match the mission.

Identify strengths such as:

- Leadership
- Creativity
- Execution
- Adaptability
- Communication
- Problem-solving

People excel when their strengths are activated.

---

4. Set High Standards and Make Them Non-Negotiable

Standards create performance.

Low standards create chaos.

High-performance teams follow standards around:

- Professionalism
- Execution
- Communication
- Accountability
- Collaboration
- Behavior

Standards separate top performers from average ones.

---

5. Hold Everyone Accountable—Equally

Accountability is the backbone of a strong team.

Leaders enforce accountability by:

- Addressing issues quickly
- Correcting behavior professionally
- Setting consequences
- Following up consistently
- Never allowing excuses to spread

A team without accountability becomes dysfunctional.

---

6. Build Trust Through Consistency

Trust is earned through actions, not words.

Teams trust leaders who:

- Keep their promises
- Follow through
- Stay consistent
- Stay fair
- Stay calm under pressure

When trust is strong, performance improves naturally.

---

7. Encourage Open, Professional Communication

High-performance teams communicate with:

- Respect
- Directness
- Transparency
- Honesty
- Alignment

Clear communication prevents confusion and builds strong collaboration.

---

8. Remove Ego From the Environment

Ego destroys teams.

It creates competition instead of collaboration.

High-performance teams put the mission first—not personal pride.

Leaders reinforce humility through:

- Shared goals
- Team recognition
- Problem-solving
- Fairness
- Equal accountability

When ego leaves, unity grows.

---

9. Give Your Team Autonomy and Ownership

People perform better when they feel trusted.

Empower your team by:

- Delegating responsibilities
- Allowing creative input
- Encouraging self-management
- Giving freedom within the standards
- Trusting them to execute

Autonomy builds confidence.

Confidence builds performance.

---

10. Create a Culture of Continuous Growth

High-performance teams are constantly improving.

Encourage growth through:

- Training
- Feedback
- Skill development

- Mentorship
- New challenges

Growth-minded teams stay motivated and competitive.

---

11. Recognize Excellence Consistently

People repeat behaviors that get recognized.

Celebrate:

- Effort
- Improvement
- Discipline
- Teamwork
- Leadership
- Achievements

Recognition boosts morale and strengthens performance.

---

12. Address Toxicity Immediately

Nothing destroys a high-performance team faster than toxic behavior.

Toxic behaviors include:

- Gossip
- Laziness
- Disrespect
- Excuses
- Drama
- Negative attitudes

Leaders must remove toxicity before it spreads.

---

13. Encourage Healthy Conflict and Problem-Solving

Conflict is not bad—it's a tool.

Healthy conflict leads to stronger ideas, better solutions, and deeper collaboration.

High-performance teams handle conflict with:

- Respect
- Logic
- Open conversation
- Solutions in mind

Avoiding conflict weakens teams—resolving conflict strengthens them.

---

14. Maintain Structure and Systems

Systems create consistency and efficiency.

High-performance teams operate with systems for:

- Communication
- Workflow
- Accountability
- Decision-making
- Problem-solving

Structure eliminates chaos and increases productivity.

---

15. Protect Team Morale

High morale increases:

- Productivity
- Creativity
- Loyalty
- Collaboration
- Energy

Leaders protect morale through:

- Fairness
- Recognition
- Clarity
- Support

- Positive culture

A motivated team performs at a higher level.

---

16. High-Performance Teams Don't Just Work Hard—They Work Smart

Efficiency is as important as effort.

High-performance teams:

- Prioritize tasks
- Manage time wisely
- Eliminate distractions
- Use resources well
- Focus on high-impact actions

Smart work multiplies results.

---

17. Create Leaders, Not Followers

A high-performance team is full of people who can lead when necessary.

Develop leaders by:

- Giving responsibility
- Teaching decision-making
- Encouraging initiative
- Building confidence
- Reinforcing accountability

A team of leaders is unstoppable.

A high-performance team is a reflection of the leader who built it.

When you create the right culture, set the right standards, and empower the right people, success becomes inevitable.

Teams win championships—

leaders build the teams that win them.

CHAPTER 38 — Managing Time Like a CEO

Time is the most valuable asset a leader has. Unlike money, once time is spent, it can never be recovered. CEOs understand that their success is directly connected to how well they manage their hours, energy, and focus. They don't just "use" time—they **control** it. They structure their days with intention, discipline, and strategy.

Average people waste time.

High-level leaders invest time.

Managing time like a CEO is not about being busy—it's about being effective.

It's about maximizing productivity, minimizing distraction, and directing your attention toward things that move your mission forward.

---

1. Time Management Starts With Clear Priorities

You cannot manage time without knowing what matters most.

CEOs prioritize based on:

- Impact
- Urgency
- Long-term value
- Mission alignment
- Efficiency

The question is never "What do I need to do today?"

It's "What will produce the greatest return for my future?"

---

2. The CEO Mindset Focuses on High-Value Tasks

Not all tasks are equal.

High-level leaders prioritize:

- Planning

- Strategy
- Relationships
- Problem-solving
- Decision-making
- Growth activities

Low-value tasks get delegated, automated, or eliminated.

Time is too precious to waste on tasks that do not elevate your mission.

---

3. CEOs Protect Their Time Ruthlessly

Most people let anyone interrupt their focus.

Leaders protect their attention like a fortress.

They limit:

- Unnecessary conversations
- Idle social media scrolling
- Unplanned meetings
- Emotional distractions
- Time-wasting environments

Your time is your power—protect it aggressively.

---

4. Create a Daily Structure That Supports Your Mission

Structure creates productivity.

Chaos destroys it.

CEOs rely on daily routines such as:

- Morning focus sessions
- Scheduled planning time
- Clear work blocks
- Meeting windows
- Breaks for recovery
- End-of-day review

A structured day produces consistent results.

---

5. Use the "Two-Hour Power Block"

Every day, leaders set aside a block of time with:

- No calls
- No meetings
- No messages
- No interruptions

This time is used for the most important task of the day.

Two hours of focused work can produce more results than 10 hours of scattered effort.

---

6. Control Your Morning, Control Your Day

Mornings set the tone.

CEOs start their day with:

- Clarity
- Planning
- Organization
- Energy renewal
- High-value tasks

They do not begin the day reacting—they begin leading.

---

7. Focus on One Task at a Time

Multitasking destroys productivity.

It weakens focus, increases mistakes, and drains mental energy.

High performers practice **deep work**:

- One task
- One focus
- One objective

Completion is more powerful than multitasking.

---

8. Limit Meetings—and Make Them Efficient

Meetings can be the biggest time-waster if not managed properly.

CEO-style meetings are:

- Short
- Focused
- Purpose-driven
- Structured
- Action-oriented

If a meeting doesn't need to happen, it doesn't happen.

---

9. Learn to Say "No" Without Apology

Every "yes" steals time from your mission.

Leaders say "no" to:

- Distractions
- Time-wasting requests
- Drama
- Unnecessary obligations
- Anything misaligned with the vision

"No" is a leadership skill.

---

10. Delegate Everything That Doesn't Require Your Expertise

Leaders don't try to do everything.

They free themselves by trusting others.

Delegate tasks that:

- Are repetitive
- Are time-consuming
- Others can do well
- Do not require your skill
- Do not contribute to the top-level mission

Delegation increases your time, your energy, and your impact.

---

11. Organize Your Environment to Support Productivity

Your environment influences your performance.

A productivity-focused environment includes:

- Clean workspace
- Tools within reach
- No clutter
- Reduced noise
- Limited distractions
- Positive energy

A clear environment creates a clear mind.

---

12. Track Your Time to Increase Awareness

You cannot improve what you do not measure.

Tracking helps you identify:

- Time leaks
- Inefficiencies
- Distractions
- Energy patterns
- Productivity strengths

Awareness is the first step to improvement.

---

13. Use Technology to Automate Your Routine

Automation saves time.

Use tools for:

- Scheduling
- Reminders
- Repetitive tasks
- Organization
- Data tracking

Automation frees your mind for more important work.

---

14. Protect Your Energy, Not Just Your Hours

Time management is also energy management.

Leaders optimize energy by:

- Taking breaks
- Eating well
- Staying hydrated
- Exercising
- Sleeping properly
- Avoiding draining people

A strong mind and body create strong performance.

---

15. Review Your Day Every Evening

Reflection sharpens performance.

At the end of the day, ask:

- "What did I achieve?"
- "What needs improvement?"
- "What distracted me?"
- "What is my top goal for tomorrow?"

Leaders end each day with intention, not exhaustion.

---

16. The Goal Is Not Just Productivity—It Is EFFECTIVENESS

Busy doesn't build success.

Results do.

Managing time like a CEO means focusing on:

- Strategic progress
- High-impact work
- Consistency
- Momentum
- Long-term success

Effectiveness creates growth.

Productivity creates motion.

Managing your time like a CEO transforms you from reactive to proactive, from overwhelmed to organized, from busy to powerful.

Your future depends on how you use your hours today.

Lead your time—

or your time will lead you.

CHAPTER 39 — Strategic Decision-Making Under Pressure

Leadership is defined in moments of pressure.

When the environment is tense, when time is limited, when emotions are high, when the risks are real—*that* is when the true strength of a leader is revealed. CEOs are not measured by how they perform when everything is easy, but by how they think, act, and decide when everything is on the line.

Strategic decision-making under pressure requires clarity, control, confidence, and logic.

It requires the ability to stay calm when others panic.

It requires the discipline to slow your thinking down when life tries to speed it up.

Pressure does not create leaders—

it *exposes* them.

---

1. Pressure Demands Emotional Control

The first rule of decision-making under pressure is simple:

Stay calm.

When emotions rise, intelligence drops.

Leaders maintain their composure because they know that emotional decisions create long-term problems.

Calmness is not weakness—it is leadership power.

---

2. Slow Down Your Thinking

Pressure tries to force quick, reactive decisions.

Strong leaders slow down long enough to think with logic.

Ask yourself:

- "What's actually happening?"
- "What are the facts?"
- "What problem am I really solving?"
- "What decision gives the best long-term outcome?"

Slowing your thoughts sharpens your clarity.

---

3. Gather Facts—Not Feelings

Feelings create confusion.

Facts create strategy.

In pressure moments, ask for:

- Data
- Evidence
- Information
- Direct reports
- Clear details
- Confirmed truth

Facts prevent emotional decisions.

---

4. Identify the Core Problem, Not the Symptoms

Pressure creates noise.

Noise hides the real issue.

Strong leaders dig deep to find the *root* of the problem, not just what's visible on the surface.

When you solve the root, everything else falls into place.

---

5. Think Long-Term, Even Under Pressure

Most people panic and think short-term: "What will fix this right now?"

Leaders think differently:

"What decision protects the mission long-term?"

Short-term solutions can create long-term damage.

Strategic leaders stay aligned with their vision even under stress.

---

6. Use the "Three Options Rule"

Under pressure, leaders avoid tunnel vision by generating multiple options.

Ask:

- "What are my three best choices?"
- "What are the pros and cons of each?"
- "Which aligns with our long-term strategy?"

Options create clarity and reduce fear.

---

7. Remove Ego From the Decision

Ego leads to:

- Defensiveness
- Emotion
- Pride-based decisions
- Avoiding responsibility
- Poor judgment

Under pressure, ego is dangerous.

Leaders choose what's *right*—not what makes them feel right.

---

8. Anticipate Consequences Before Acting

Strong decision-makers think ahead.

Ask:

- "What happens if I choose this?"
- "Who does this affect?"
- "What could go wrong?"
- "What could go right?"
- "What doors does this open or close?"

Forward thinking prevents regret.

---

9. Seek Advice From Trusted Voices—Not Too Many Voices

Leaders do not isolate themselves.

But they also do not let too many opinions cloud their mind.

Seek counsel from:

- Experienced mentors
- Rational thinkers
- People with no emotional agenda
- Subject-matter experts

A few strong perspectives are better than many loud ones.

---

10. Maintain Professionalism Regardless of Stress

Pressure exposes people.

Some get emotional.

Some get reactive.

Some get disrespectful.

Leaders remain:

- Calm
- Respectful
- Clear
- Direct
- Controlled

Professionalism under pressure earns trust and respect.

---

11. Trust Your Preparation and Experience

Decision-making becomes easier when you trust:

- Your knowledge
- Your instincts
- Your training

- Your past experiences
- Your leadership presence

Confidence comes from preparation.

Leaders rely on their preparation in moments of pressure.

---

12. Act Decisively—Avoid Hesitation

Indecision is still a decision—and usually the wrong one.

Once you have the facts and clarity, choose the best path and commit.

Leaders don't freeze.

They move forward with confidence.

---

13. Adjust When Necessary—Don't Be Afraid to Pivot

A strong leader is decisive,

but also flexible.

If new information arises.

If the situation changes.

If the strategy stops working…

A pivot is not weakness—it's intelligence.

Adaptability makes you unstoppable.

---

14. Communicate Your Decision Clearly

Unclear communication turns good decisions into chaos.

A strong leader explains:

- What the decision is
- Why it was made
- What the next steps are
- Who is responsible
- What the expected outcome is

Clarity aligns everyone.

---

15. Own the Outcome Without Excuses

Leaders take full responsibility for:

- Success
- Mistakes
- Unintended consequences
- Next steps

Ownership builds trust.

Excuses destroy it.

---

16. Evaluate the Decision After the Pressure Passes

Every decision—good or bad—teaches a lesson.

After the situation settles, ask:

- "What did I learn?"
- "What would I do differently?"
- "How can I strengthen my process?"
- "What patterns should I note for the future?"

Reflection sharpens wisdom.

Strategic decision-making under pressure is not a talent.

It is a skill—developed through discipline, experience, and emotional control.

Leaders who master this skill become trustworthy, influential, and unshakeable.

They guide others through uncertainty with clarity and strength.

They rise higher because they stay calm when others break.

Pressure does not define great leaders—

their decisions do.

CHAPTER 40 — The CEO Approach to Problem-Solving

Every leader faces problems.

Every business faces obstacles.

Every dream encounters challenges.

But CEOs separate themselves because they don't panic, complain, or avoid issues—they solve them with clarity, structure, and strategic thinking.

Problems are not interruptions to leadership—

they are the proving grounds of leadership.

A CEO's value comes from their ability to take complex issues, break them down, and create clear solutions that move the mission forward.

Problem-solving is not just a skill—

it is one of the core responsibilities of leadership.

---

1. CEOs See Problems as Information, Not Threats

Average people get emotional when problems appear.

Leaders get analytical.

They ask:

- "What is this situation trying to show me?"
- "Where did this come from?"
- "What can I learn from this?"

Problems become opportunities when you remove the emotion.

---

2. Define the Real Problem Before Acting

Most people waste time fixing symptoms instead of solving the root issue.

Effective problem-solvers ask:

- "What is the root cause?"
- "What is really happening beneath the surface?"
- "What is the true breakdown?"

Clarity prevents wasted effort.

---

3. Gather All Relevant Information

You cannot solve what you do not fully understand.

Gather:

- Facts
- Data
- Reports
- Perspectives
- Evidence
- Timeline details

Knowing the full picture gives you power.

---

4. Break the Problem Into Smaller Parts

A big problem feels overwhelming until it's broken down.

Divide the issue into:

- Components
- Causes
- Steps
- Key players
- Timeline points

Small pieces make big problems manageable.

---

5. Don't React Emotionally—Respond Strategically

Emotion destroys logic.

Strategy restores control.

CEOs take a moment to:

- Breathe
- Think
- Analyze
- Reframe
- Focus

Strategic responses prevent emotional mistakes.

---

6. Use the "Five Why" Method

This method gets to the root cause fast.

Ask "Why?" five times until the real issue appears.

Example:

Problem: "The project failed."

Why? "The deadline was missed."

Why? "The team didn't communicate."

Why? "There was no process."

Why? "Expectations weren't clear."

Why? "Leadership didn't set them."

The root problem becomes clear.

---

7. Identify Every Possible Solution

Leaders do not settle for the first idea—they generate multiple options.

Ask:

- "What are three solutions?"
- "What is the fastest fix?"
- "What is the long-term solution?"
- "What are creative alternatives?"

Options increase clarity.

---

8. Evaluate Each Solution with Logic, Not Emotion

Every solution has:

- Pros
- Cons
- Risks
- Resources needed
- Time required
- Impact level

Leaders choose solutions based on long-term value, not temporary convenience.

---

9. Choose the Solution That Protects the Mission

Some solutions are easy.

Some are fast.

Some are comfortable.

But CEOs choose the solution that:

- Supports the long-term vision
- Strengthens the culture
- Builds stability
- Increases effectiveness
- Aligns with the mission

Mission first—comfort second.

---

10. Create an Action Plan With Clear Steps

A solution is meaningless without execution.

Your action plan must include:

- Who is responsible
- What will be done
- When it will be completed

- What resources are needed
- What success looks like

Action creates progress.

---

11. Communicate the Plan Clearly

The team must understand:

- The decision
- The process
- The expectations
- The timeline
- The responsibilities

Clear communication aligns everyone toward the solution.

---

12. Execute With Focus and Consistency

Strong leaders don't abandon solutions midway.

They push until the problem is resolved.

Execution requires:

- Commitment
- Follow-through
- Accountability
- Consistent evaluation

Solutions fail when leaders stop too early.

---

13. Monitor Progress and Adjust When Needed

Every solution requires oversight.

Leaders:

- Track results
- Address new issues
- Adjust the strategy

- Reassign tasks if necessary
- Stay flexible

Adaptation strengthens the outcome.

---

14. Document the Process

Documentation prevents repeated mistakes and builds organizational intelligence.

Record:

- What the problem was
- What caused it
- How it was solved
- What improvements were made
- What should be done next time

Leaders build systems from experience.

---

15. Reflect, Learn, and Improve

Every problem leaves behind wisdom.

Ask:

- "What did this teach me?"
- "What patterns do I need to watch for?"
- "How can I prevent this from happening again?"
- "What new system needs to be built?"

Reflection strengthens leadership.

---

16. Teach Your Team How to Solve Problems

The best leaders don't solve every problem themselves—

they *build problem-solvers.*

Show your team how to:

- Analyze issues
- Think critically

- Stay calm
- Ask the right questions
- Create solutions

A team of problem-solvers is unstoppable.

Problems are not the enemy of leadership—

they are the pathway to mastery.

Every problem you solve increases your confidence, strengthens your leadership, and expands your influence.

Problems build resilience, sharpen thinking, and refine character.

The CEO approach to problem-solving turns chaos into clarity, obstacles into opportunities, and challenges into growth.

Leaders are not defined by the problems they face—

but by the solutions they create.

CHAPTER 41 — The Power of Consistency and Momentum

Success is not built on motivation—

it is built on **consistency**.

Momentum is not created in one big moment—

it is created through small, steady actions repeated over time.

Every CEO, every high performer, every elite leader understands this truth:

Consistency beats intensity.

A little progress done daily beats massive effort done occasionally.

Consistency builds confidence.

Momentum builds power.

Together, they make you unstoppable.

---

1. Consistency Is the Foundation of All Achievement

One workout does not make you strong.

One effort does not create mastery.

One good day does not build a successful life.

But consistency does.

Great leaders operate like this:

- They show up even when they don't feel like it.
- They practice discipline daily.
- They commit to routines.
- They build habits that support their goals.
- They stay on the path long after motivation fades.

Consistency is commitment in action.

---

2. Momentum Is Created by Repeated Movement

Momentum is the feeling of progress accelerating.

It happens when your effort compounds.

You start seeing:

- Faster results
- Sharper skills
- Easier decisions
- More opportunities
- Higher confidence

Momentum turns discipline into power.

---

3. Small Daily Wins Matter More Than Big Occasional Wins

Most people wait for perfect conditions before acting.

Leaders understand that progress comes from doing *something* every day.

Small wins include:

- Reading a few pages
- Sending that one email
- Making that one call
- Improving one system
- Learning one new insight
- Completing one new task

Small wins keep you moving.

Movement builds momentum.

---

4. Eliminate "Start-Stop" Behavior

The biggest killer of momentum is inconsistency.

Start-stop behavior includes:

- Working hard one week, quitting the next

- Being disciplined Monday–Wednesday, then falling off
- Starting new goals but never finishing
- Getting motivated, losing motivation, then restarting from zero

Start-stop cycles destroy progress.

Consistency multiplies it.

---

5. Build Habits That Support Your Vision

Habits automate success.

High performers focus on building:

- Morning routines
- Daily planning habits
- Clear work blocks
- Learning habits
- Health routines
- Accountability systems

Habits remove decision fatigue and make consistency easier.

---

6. Remove Distractions That Break Your Rhythm

Momentum requires focus.

Distractions destroy focus.

Common momentum killers:

- Negative people
- Social media overload
- Procrastination
- Overthinking
- Toxic environments
- Poor planning

Protect your focus like a valuable asset—it is.

---

7. Track Your Progress to Stay Motivated

What gets measured gets improved.

Tracking gives you:

- Motivation
- Insight
- Accountability
- Clarity
- Proof of progress

Seeing results builds belief.

Belief fuels discipline.

---

8. Keep Showing Up Even When You Don't Feel Like It

Feelings are inconsistent.

Discipline is reliable.

Some of your best progress will be made on days when you didn't feel motivated at all.

Motivation creates movement.

Discipline creates results.

---

9. Stay Patient—Momentum Builds Slowly at First

The beginning is the hardest part.

You may feel like:

- You're working hard with little progress
- Nothing is happening
- It's taking too long
- Others are moving faster

But consistency is building something underneath the surface.

Success compounds quietly—

then suddenly.

---

10. Increase Your Pace Gradually

Momentum grows with time.

Start small, then build:

- Add five more minutes
- Do one more task
- Improve one small area
- Increase intensity slowly

Let your momentum rise naturally.

Forced momentum breaks.

Natural momentum compounds.

---

11. Surround Yourself With Consistent People

Your environment shapes your habits.

Success grows around:

- Disciplined people
- Focused individuals
- Driven minds
- Growth-oriented teams
- High standards
- Positive influence

Energy is contagious—pick the right environment.

---

12. Use Rest Strategically to Avoid Burnout

Consistency requires sustainability.

Rest is a strategic part of momentum.

Not quitting—resting.

Not giving up—resetting.

Leaders balance:

- Intensity
- Recovery
- Focus

- Reflection

Rest strengthens your consistency.

---

13. Momentum Makes Hard Things Easier

Once momentum builds, everything feels smoother.

You start to:

- Work faster
- Think clearer
- Decide quicker
- Learn faster
- Perform better

Momentum is a force that pushes you forward without extra effort.

---

14. Consistency Turns Ordinary People Into Extraordinary Leaders

You don't need to be the smartest, the fastest, or the most talented.

Consistency and momentum outperform talent every time.

The people who win long-term are the ones who:

- Keep going
- Stay disciplined
- Don't quit
- Build strong habits
- Maintain their pace
- Believe in long-term results

Consistency creates mastery.

Momentum fuels greatness.

---

15. Success Belongs to the Consistent, Not the Occasional

Anyone can be great for a moment.

Few remain great consistently.

The leaders who rise to the top do so because they refuse to break their momentum.

Day after day.

Week after week.

Year after year.

Consistency becomes identity.

Momentum becomes power.

Success becomes lifestyle.

Consistency is the engine.

Momentum is the acceleration.

Together, they create unstoppable leaders.

CHAPTER 42 — Building Influence and Leadership Presence

Leadership isn't just about titles, authority, or position.

True leadership is about **influence**—your ability to impact how people think, feel, act, and perform. Leadership presence is the energy you project, the respect you command, and the confidence you inspire when you enter a room.

Some people speak, and no one listens.

Others speak, and everyone pays attention.

That is leadership presence.

Influence is not forced.

It is earned—through consistency, strength, clarity, and character.

When you build leadership presence, people trust you, follow you, and rise under your direction.

---

1. Presence Begins With Confidence

Confidence is silent power.

It's not arrogance or ego—it's self-assurance rooted in discipline and preparation.

Leadership confidence comes from:

- Knowing your purpose
- Trusting your abilities
- Standing firm in your values
- Keeping your promises
- Staying calm under pressure

Confidence makes people feel safe following you.

---

2. Influence Requires Emotional Control

People follow leaders who remain steady.

You cannot influence anyone if you:

- Overreact
- Get offended easily
- Lose your temper
- Panic under pressure
- Make emotional decisions

Emotional control is leadership control.

---

3. Speak With Clarity and Authority

Leaders don't mumble.

They don't ramble.

They don't sound unsure.

Your communication must be:

- Strong
- Clear
- Direct
- Confident
- Purposeful

When you speak with authority, people listen with respect.

---

4. Your Energy Introduces You Before Your Words Do

Leadership presence is felt before it's heard.

Your energy communicates:

- Confidence
- Strength
- Professionalism
- Respect
- Purpose

This is why posture, eye contact, tone, and body language matter.

---

5. Influence Comes From Integrity

People will not follow a leader they cannot trust.

Integrity includes:

- Honesty
- Consistency
- Accountability
- Transparency
- Strong values

Your character is your leadership identity.

---

6. Be the Example, Not the Exception

The most powerful leaders live the standards they expect.

They:

- Show up on time
- Work hard
- Communicate clearly
- Stay disciplined
- Honor their commitments

People follow what you *do*, not what you say.

---

7. Build Trust Through Consistency

Trust is the foundation of influence.

You build trust by being:

- Reliable
- Predictable
- Honest
- Fair
- Steady in your behavior

A leader who changes constantly loses influence quickly.

---

8. Influence Grows Through Listening

Influence is not about talking more—it's about understanding more.

Strong leaders listen to:

- Concerns
- Ideas
- Feedback
- Emotions
- Challenges

Listening builds connection, and connection builds influence.

---

9. Leadership Presence Requires Professionalism

Professionalism separates leaders from the crowd.

This includes:

- Respectful communication
- Controlled behavior
- Clean appearance
- Strong work ethic
- Mature decision-making

Professionalism commands respect without demanding it.

---

10. Show Strength Without Being Intimidating

True power is calm, not loud.

Leaders don't need to yell, dominate, or control.

Their presence alone sets the tone.

Strength shows through:

- Confidence
- Boundaries
- Composure
- Consistency

- Calm leadership

People follow strong leaders—not aggressive ones.

---

11. Be Clear About Your Values and Standards

Influence is rooted in identity.

You build strong presence when people know what you stand for:

- Honor
- Respect
- Discipline
- Excellence
- Accountability

Your values become your leadership fingerprint.

---

12. Provide Value Wherever You Go

Influencers add value—

not noise, gossip, or negativity.

Value includes:

- Solutions
- Ideas
- Encouragement
- Strategy
- Leadership

People respect the voice that brings value.

---

13. Stay Humble While Remaining Confident

Humility keeps your influence relatable.

Confidence keeps you authoritative.

The balance of both makes you magnetic.

Humble leaders earn loyalty.

Confident leaders earn respect.

Together, they create unstoppable influence.

---

14. Influence Requires Consistent Self-Improvement

Leaders grow—

and because they grow, people trust their direction.

Self-improvement includes:

- Reading
- Training
- Mentorship
- Study
- Reflection
- Skill development

Growth strengthens presence.

---

15. Handle Conflict With Strength and Class

Your leadership presence is revealed in tension.

When conflict arises:

- Stay calm
- Listen professionally
- Communicate clearly
- Solve the issue
- Avoid emotional reactions

People follow the leader who stays strong when others break.

---

16. Own Your Decisions Without Hesitation

Indecision weakens influence.

Leaders who stand by their decisions with confidence and clarity build trust.

Even if the decision isn't perfect, ownership inspires respect.

---

17. Influence Requires Consistency Across Every Space

Your presence must be the same:

- In public
- In private
- At work
- At home
- With your team
- With your peers

Consistency builds leadership identity.

Influence is not given—it is earned.

Leadership presence is not natural—it is developed.

People follow leaders who show strength, confidence, clarity, and integrity every day.

When you build influence and presence,

you command attention without asking for it.

You inspire action without forcing it.

You create impact with your words, energy, and example.

This is the power of a true leader.

CHAPTER 43 — Leading With Purpose and Vision

(Expanded Version)

Leadership without purpose is directionless.

Leadership without vision is powerless.

The greatest CEOs, founders, and world changers lead with a purpose that inspires them and a vision that directs them. Purpose fuels the heart. Vision guides the mind. Together, they create leaders who can withstand challenges, influence others, and build something meaningful.

Purpose answers **why** you lead.

Vision answers **where** you are going.

Strategy answers **how** you will get there.

When a leader operates with all three, they become magnetic, powerful, and unforgettable.

---

1. Purpose Is the Fire That Drives Leadership

Purpose is not a goal—it is the deeply rooted reason behind your goals.

Purpose comes from:

- What you care about
- What drives you
- What you want to change
- What you want to build
- What impact you want to leave

Purpose gives meaning to your work and strength to your leadership.

---

2. Vision Gives You Direction and Focus

Vision is the long-term picture of what you want to create.

A leader's vision should be:

- Clear
- Big
- Inspiring
- Strategic
- Worth pursuing

Vision is your destination.

Without it, your leadership feels lost.

---

3. Purpose Creates Passion—Vision Creates Alignment

Purpose motivates **you**.

Vision motivates **your team**.

Purpose fuels your energy during hard moments.

Vision keeps everyone united during the journey.

Both are necessary for long-term success.

---

4. Your Vision Must Be Bigger Than Your Fear

If your vision doesn't scare you a little, it's too small.

Great leaders have visions that stretch them, challenge them, and push them outside their comfort zone.

Fear protects small thinkers.

Vision guides leaders.

---

5. Leaders Communicate Vision Clearly and Often

A vision that isn't communicated is a vision that dies.

Effective leaders communicate their vision:

- Consistently
- Passionately
- Confidently
- Clearly

- With direction and expectation

People follow leaders who help them *see* the future.

---

6. Purpose Creates Endurance During Hard Times

Leadership brings challenges.

Obstacles.

Pressure.

Unexpected setbacks.

Purpose gives you emotional and mental endurance.

Purpose reminds you:

"Don't quit. You're meant for this."

Without purpose, leaders break.

With purpose, they rise.

---

7. Vision Requires Daily Alignment

A vision doesn't just guide the future—it guides daily actions.

Leaders ask:

"Does this action align with my vision?"

"Does this decision get me closer to my goal?"

"Is this energy supporting or distracting me?"

Vision eliminates distractions and keeps the leader focused.

---

8. Purpose and Vision Must Be Backed by Values

Values are the guardrails of leadership.

They define:

- How you behave
- How you lead
- What you tolerate
- What you refuse

- What you expect

Leaders with strong values inspire trust.

---

9. Your Team Must Feel Connected to the Vision

People don't follow tasks—they follow missions.

To build unity:

- Explain why the mission matters
- Show how each person contributes
- Recognize progress
- Create shared goals
- Celebrate milestones

When the team feels ownership, the vision becomes powerful.

---

10. Vision Requires Courageous Decisions

Great visions demand bold choices.

Sometimes you must:

- Take risks
- Pivot strategy
- Reject comfort
- Make unpopular decisions
- Step into the unknown

Leaders make decisions that their vision requires—not what their comfort desires.

---

11. Purpose Shapes Your Leadership Identity

Purpose defines:

- Your communication style
- Your leadership tone
- Your passion

- Your resilience
- Your authenticity

Purpose makes you relatable and human.

---

12. Vision Must Be Reviewed and Refined Over Time

Life changes.

Opportunities change.

Strategies change.

Vision may stay the same, but the path can evolve.

Review your vision consistently to ensure it stays sharp and aligned with your growth.

---

13. Leading With Purpose Attracts the Right People

People want to follow leaders who:

- Stand for something
- Believe in something
- Fight for something
- Build something bigger than themselves

Purpose attracts loyalty.

Vision attracts talent.

Alignment attracts momentum.

---

14. Purpose Creates Legacy

Purpose-driven leaders create more than results—they create impact.

Legacy is built by leaders who:

- Inspire growth
- Change lives
- Build people
- Serve their mission

- Stand firm in their values

Legacy is the highest form of leadership.

---

15. Vision Turns Ordinary Leadership Into Extraordinary Impact

Vision gives your leadership:

- Power
- Direction
- Magnetism
- Influence
- Meaning

It turns a single leader into a movement.

Purpose is the heart of leadership.

Vision is the eyes of leadership.

Together, they create leadership that changes lives, shapes futures, and transforms environments.

When you lead with purpose and vision, you build more than success—

you build significance.

CHAPTER 44 — Financial Discipline and Wealth Leadership

Money does not make a leader—

but financial discipline absolutely does.

Great leaders understand money, manage money, and multiply money.

Financial discipline is not about being cheap—

it's about being **strategic**, **organized**, and **focused** on long-term stability and wealth.

Wealth leadership is the ability to:

- Control your finances
- Make intelligent money decisions
- Reduce unnecessary risk
- Build long-term assets
- Lead your organization or household with financial clarity

A leader who cannot manage money cannot manage growth.

Financial discipline is leadership discipline.

---

1. Financial Leadership Begins With Awareness

You cannot improve what you do not track.

Leaders know:

- Where money is going
- What they're spending on
- What their priorities are
- What their obligations are
- What their long-term financial picture looks like

Awareness is the first step toward wealth.

---

2. Create a Clear, Simple Budget That Aligns With Your Goals

A budget is not restriction—it's direction.

It tells your money where to go instead of wondering where it went.

Strong financial leaders budget for:

- Essentials
- Investments
- Emergencies
- Debt management
- Growth opportunities
- Personal development

A budget is the roadmap of your financial vision.

---

3. Separate Wants From Needs

Leaders understand the difference between:

- What feels good
- What builds stability
- What creates long-term wealth

Discipline means saying **no** to short-term pleasure to gain long-term freedom.

---

4. Build an Emergency Fund to Protect Yourself From Crisis

Life happens.

Emergencies come.

Unexpected costs appear.

Leaders prepare so they never panic.

An emergency fund gives you:

- Security
- Stability
- Confidence

- Options
- Peace of mind

Preparedness is power.

---

5. Reduce Debt Strategically and Aggressively

Debt is a weight that slows progress.

Leaders face debt with strategy—not fear or avoidance.

Effective debt leadership includes:

- Listing all debts
- Understanding interest rates
- Targeting the highest interest first
- Building a payoff plan
- Cutting habits that increase debt

Financial freedom begins with financial responsibility.

---

6. Invest in Assets—Not Liabilities

Liabilities take money out of your pocket.

Assets put money into your pocket.

Assets include:

- Stocks
- Real estate
- Businesses
- Intellectual property
- Skillsets
- Savings growth
- Passive income streams

Wealth grows from what you build—
not what you buy.

---

7. Always Pay Yourself First

Before bills.

Before expenses.

Before spending.

The first payment should be:

- Savings
- Investments
- Future growth

Leaders prioritize their future over temporary impulse.

---

8. Live Below Your Means to Grow Above Your Circumstances

This doesn't mean living small—

it means living smart.

Financial discipline gives you:

- Flexibility
- Stability
- Choice
- Freedom

The more disciplined you are, the more options you create.

---

9. Build Multiple Streams of Income

Relying on one source of income is financial risk.

Leaders diversify.

Income streams can include:

- Side businesses
- Rental property
- Dividends
- Digital products
- Consulting or coaching
- Royalties

- Service-based income

Multiple income streams build financial protection and long-term power.

---

10. Make Money Decisions Based on Logic, Not Emotion

Emotional spending destroys financial progress.

Leaders ask:

- "Does this align with my goals?"
- "Do I need this, or do I want it?"
- "Does this purchase build wealth, or drain it?"
- "What will this decision cost me later?"

Logic builds wealth.

Emotion destroys it.

---

11. Use Financial Tools and Systems to Stay Organized

Successful leaders use:

- Budgets
- Calendars
- Financial apps
- Automatic savings
- Automatic bill payments
- Debt tracking systems

Systems protect you from inconsistency.

---

12. Understand Taxes, Credit, and Interest

Leaders don't ignore financial literacy—

they study it.

They understand:

- How taxes work
- How credit affects opportunities

- The cost of interest
- How to leverage credit responsibly

A financially educated leader is a financially powerful leader.

---

13. Protect Your Wealth With Insurance and Planning

Wealth is built by discipline but protected by preparation.

This includes:

- Life insurance
- Health insurance
- Business insurance
- Asset protection
- Retirement planning
- Estate planning

Protection prevents disaster.

---

14. Surround Yourself With Financially Wise People

Your financial environment matters.

Learn from those who:

- Invest
- Grow
- Save
- Build
- Create
- Expand

Financial maturity grows in a financially mature environment.

---

15. Teach Financial Responsibility to the People You Lead

Real leadership passes down wisdom.

Teach your team, family, or business how to:

- Budget
- Save

- Invest
- Make smart decisions
- Build long-term stability

Leaders build leaders—not dependents.

---

16. Wealth Leadership Requires Long-Term Thinking

The greatest financial discipline is patience.

Choose long-term security over short-term pleasure.

Choose assets over status.

Choose growth over impulse.

Choose future freedom over temporary excitement.

That is wealth leadership.

Financial discipline is not about money—

it's about structure, character, and long-term thinking.

When you lead your finances with purpose, clarity, and consistency, you create a life of freedom, stability, and opportunity.

Wealth is not luck.

Wealth is leadership.

CHAPTER 45 — Elevating Your Team to High Performance

(Expanded Version)

A leader is only as strong as the team they build.

High-performance teams don't appear by accident—

they are built through intentional leadership, clear standards, consistent accountability, and a culture that pushes people to grow.

A great leader doesn't just manage people.

A great leader **elevates** people.

Your team should get better because of your leadership.

Your presence should increase their focus, discipline, and confidence.

Your standards should raise their performance and expectations of themselves.

High-performance teams follow high-performance leaders.

---

1. Set Clear Standards From the Beginning

People cannot perform at a high level if they don't know what high performance looks like.

Standards must be:

- Clear
- Simple
- Direct
- Non-negotiable
- Consistently communicated

Confusion destroys performance.

Clarity strengthens it.

---

2. Create a Culture of Accountability

High-performance teams hold themselves and each other accountable.

Accountability means:

- Owning your role
- Meeting expectations
- Delivering results
- Being responsible for outcomes
- Avoiding excuses

A team with accountability becomes unstoppable.

---

3. Communicate With Consistency and Precision

High-performance teams don't guess—they know.

Great leaders communicate:

- Directly
- Respectfully
- Professionally
- With clarity and purpose

The more clear the message, the higher the performance.

---

4. Develop the Strengths of Each Team Member

Every team member has unique strengths.

Leaders elevate performance by:

- Recognizing strengths
- Assigning tasks based on ability
- Providing opportunities for growth
- Encouraging specialization
- Helping people develop confidence

People perform best when they operate in their strengths.

---

5. Address Weaknesses With Guidance, Not Condemnation

Weakness is not failure—it is an opportunity to coach.

Leaders help team members improve by:

- Identifying skill gaps
- Providing training
- Offering feedback
- Being patient
- Setting improvement goals

Strong leaders build strong people.

---

6. Provide Consistent Feedback—Positive and Corrective

Feedback is fuel.

Positive feedback builds confidence.

Corrective feedback builds discipline.

High-performance teams need both.

Great leaders give feedback that is:

- Honest
- Specific
- Respectful
- Growth-focused
- Actionable

Feedback keeps performance sharp.

---

7. Lead By Example—Always

Your team mirrors your behavior.

If you want:

- Discipline
- Excellence
- Professionalism
- Consistency
- Focus

- Strong character

You must model it daily.

Leadership is influence through example.

---

8. Create an Environment Where Hard Work Is Normal

High-performance teams thrive in environments where:

- Everyone pushes themselves
- Excellence is expected
- Complaining is discouraged
- Results matter
- Growth is continuous

Culture sets the tone.

Leaders set the culture.

---

9. Remove Toxicity Immediately

Nothing destroys performance quicker than:

- Negativity
- Drama
- Laziness
- Gossip
- Undermining behavior
- Disrespect

Leaders protect the culture fiercely.

A high-performance environment cannot tolerate low-performance behavior.

---

10. Build Trust Through Consistency

Trust creates safe communication and maximum performance.

Trust grows when leaders are:

- Predictable
- Honest

- Fair
- Supportive
- Consistent

People perform better when they trust their leader.

---

11. Encourage Ownership of Roles

High-performance teams don't wait for directions—they take initiative.

Encourage your team to:

- Make decisions
- Solve problems
- Take responsibility
- Offer ideas
- Communicate needs

Ownership turns employees into leaders.

---

12. Provide Resources and Tools for Success

Performance improves when people have what they need.

Give your team:

- Training
- Technology
- Support
- Clear expectations
- Mentoring
- Systems

Well-equipped teams perform better.

---

13. Celebrate Wins—Small and Big

Recognition boosts morale and inspires continued effort.

Celebrate:

- Completed goals
- Team achievements
- Personal growth
- Improvements
- Milestones

Celebration strengthens culture.

---

14. Challenge Your Team With Higher Expectations

People rise to the level of expectation.

Leaders elevate performance by:

- Increasing standards
- Giving harder challenges
- Encouraging growth
- Pushing for excellence
- Holding people capable

Challenge reveals potential.

---

15. Remove Fear and Replace It With Confidence

High-performance teams don't operate from fear.

Leaders remove fear by:

- Creating a supportive environment
- Encouraging communication
- Allowing questions
- Coaching through mistakes
- Valuing development

Confidence increases performance.

---

16. Empower Future Leaders Within the Team

A great leader builds leaders—not followers.

Develop future leaders by:

- Delegating responsibility
- Teaching decision-making
- Coaching communication
- Assigning leadership roles
- Building confidence and skill

A team full of leaders is powerful.

---

17. Keep the Mission in Front of the Team

High-performance teams stay focused on the mission.

Leaders constantly reinforce:

- Why the work matters
- Who it impacts
- What the long-term goal is
- Why excellence is expected

Purpose strengthens performance.

A high-performance team doesn't happen by luck.

It happens because the leader built it with intention, clarity, vision, and discipline.

When you elevate your team, you elevate your results.

When you build strong people, you build a strong future.

Leadership is not about being powerful—it's about empowering others.

High-performance teams are built by high-performance leaders.

CHAPTER 46 — The Mental Toughness of a CEO

(Expanded Version)

Leadership at the highest level requires more than intelligence, experience, or charisma—it requires **mental toughness**. CEOs deal with pressure, uncertainty, criticism, responsibility, and decisions that impact careers, finances, and futures. The weight is heavy, and not everyone can carry it.

Mental toughness is the inner strength that keeps a leader steady when challenges hit hard. It is the ability to stay focused when distractions rise, remain calm when chaos appears, and keep moving forward when fear tries to hold you back.

Mental toughness is not about being emotionless—

it's about being **unbreakable.**

---

1. Mental Toughness Begins With Emotional Discipline

Your emotions influence your decisions, reactions, and leadership presence.

A mentally tough leader:

- Responds, not reacts
- Stays calm under pressure
- Controls their tone
- Uses logic over emotion
- Remains professional even when frustrated

Emotional discipline is leadership power.

---

2. Tough Leaders Handle Pressure Without Falling Apart

Pressure is part of the job.

Every leader faces:

- Deadlines
- Expectations
- Problems
- Conflict
- Responsibility
- Emergencies

Mentally tough leaders embrace pressure instead of running from it.

They see pressure as a sign of trust and responsibility.

---

3. They Stay Focused When Others Panic

When chaos hits, most people lose focus.

They freeze, overthink, or fall apart emotionally.

But great leaders:

- Slow their thinking
- Breathe
- Analyze the situation
- Make strategic decisions
- Maintain clarity

Focus is a superpower under stress.

---

4. They Develop Thick Skin Without Becoming Cold

Mentally tough leaders don't crumble under criticism.

They understand:

- Opinions do not define them
- Criticism is part of leadership
- Growth comes from feedback
- Not everyone will like their decisions

Thick skin protects leadership.

Emotional maturity protects relationships.

---

5. They Keep Moving Forward Even When Tired or Discouraged

Not every day will be productive.

Not every week will be easy.

Not every situation will feel good.

Mental toughness means:

- Showing up tired
- Working when unmotivated
- Staying committed when results are slow
- Moving forward when excuses tempt you

Consistency beats emotion every time.

---

6. They Master Self-Control

Leaders cannot afford:

- Outbursts
- Emotional meltdowns
- Impulsive decisions
- Dramatic reactions
- Unprofessional behavior

Self-control earns respect.

Lack of control destroys it.

---

7. They Keep Their Vision in Front, Even During Storms

Mentally tough leaders never lose sight of where they're going.

They remind themselves:

- "This is temporary."
- "The vision is bigger than the challenge."
- "Hard times are part of the journey."
- "Quitting is not an option."

Vision makes leaders unshakeable.

---

8. They Don't Take Things Personally

This is one of the highest forms of toughness.

People will:

- Complain
- Misunderstand
- Criticize
- Doubt you
- Resist change

Mentally tough leaders focus on the mission—not people's opinions.

---

9. They Learn From Mistakes Instead of Avoiding Them

Weak leaders fear mistakes.

Strong leaders grow from them.

Mistakes teach:

- Strategy
- Discipline
- Preparation
- Leadership maturity
- Better decision-making

Mistakes strengthen leaders who face them.

---

10. They Manage Stress Instead of Letting Stress Manage Them

Stress is unavoidable.

But suffering is optional.

Strong leaders manage stress by:

- Planning ahead
- Staying organized
- Taking responsibility
- Communicating early

- Using healthy coping habits

Stress becomes fuel when handled correctly.

---

11. They Use Logic When Everyone Else Uses Emotion

During emotional moments, mentally tough leaders rise above the noise.

They ask:

- "What are the facts?"
- "What is the smartest move?"
- "What is best for the mission?"

Logic creates clarity.

Clarity creates leadership strength.

---

12. They Don't Fear Difficult Conversations

Leadership requires communication that is:

- Honest
- Direct
- Respectful
- Clear
- Necessary

Weak leaders avoid tough conversations.

Strong leaders initiate them.

---

13. They Protect Their Peace From Outside Negativity

Mentally tough leaders refuse to be pulled into:

- Gossip
- Drama
- Confusion
- Chaos
- Emotional games

They stay centered, focused, and intentional.

Peace is leadership currency.

---

14. They Maintain Confidence During Uncertainty

Even when unsure, strong leaders act with confidence.

Not fake confidence—

But confidence built from:

- Competence
- Preparation
- Experience
- Faith in their ability to adapt

Uncertainty reveals leadership strength.

---

15. They Know When to Rest Without Quitting

Mental toughness includes knowing your limits.

Rest is:

- Strategic
- Necessary
- Productive
- Healthy

Quitting destroys progress.

Rest recharges leadership.

---

16. They Stay Purpose-Driven, Not Emotion-Driven

Purpose pushes you forward.

Emotion pulls you backward.

Leaders driven by purpose always rise above challenges.

Mental toughness is not about being a robot.

It is about being a **stable, reliable, disciplined leader** who can be trusted under pressure.

When you build mental toughness, you:

- Make better decisions
- Lead stronger teams
- Build confidence
- Handle challenges effectively
- Rise above average leadership

Mental toughness is what separates leaders who break from leaders who breakthrough.

CHAPTER 47 — How CEOs Think Differently From Everyone Else

Leading Through Uncertainty: How CEOs Stay Confident When the Future Isn't Clear**

Uncertainty is one of the few guarantees in leadership. Markets shift. Employees come and go. Competitors innovate overnight. Technology evolves at a pace no human can fully predict. And yet, great CEOs continue to make decisions, move forward, and inspire confidence— even when the path ahead is foggy.

This ability isn't luck. It's a skill. It's a mindset. And, more importantly, it's a discipline that separates leaders who freeze from leaders who rise.

In this chapter, we explore the CEO strategies for navigating uncertainty with strength, clarity, and resilience.

---

1. Accept That Uncertainty Is Normal—Not a Threat

Many people panic in uncertain conditions because they believe uncertainty is a sign of danger. CEOs understand something different:

Uncertainty is standard, expected, and unavoidable.

Instead of trying to eliminate it, they **learn to operate inside it**.

This shift in mindset reduces fear. It frees mental energy. And it helps you make decisions based on logic—not anxiety.

CEO Question:

Do you treat uncertainty as a threat, or as a natural part of progress?

---

2. Make Decisions with the Information You Have, Not the Information You Wish You Had

Most people wait for perfect data. CEOs move with *enough* data.

Why?

Because speed often matters more than certainty.

A decision made at 80% confidence today is usually more powerful than a decision made at 100% confidence six months too late.

CEO Principle:

Imperfect action beats perfect hesitation.

Great leaders gather what they can, think critically, and execute decisively—while staying flexible enough to pivot if new information appears.

---

3. Create Stability Through Communication

In uncertain times, employees don't need a perfect plan.

They need a **present leader**.

CEOs communicate more frequently during uncertain periods—not less.

They provide updates.

They share what is known and unknown.

They explain what actions are being taken.

They speak with calmness, strength, and clarity.

When people understand the direction, the fear decreases.

When people feel informed, they feel safe.

Communication builds confidence. Silence builds confusion.

---

4. Focus on What You Can Control

Uncertainty creates emotional overwhelm because the mind jumps to everything outside of your influence. CEOs beat this mental trap by redirecting their attention to controllable factors:

- Their decision-making
- Their attitude
- Their preparation
- Their behavior
- Their leadership presence

This creates a sense of power, even in chaos.

CEO Exercise:

Write down 3 things you *can control* in your situation right now.

Then write down 3 things you *cannot control*.

Let go of the second list. Take action on the first.

---

5. Build Flexible Strategies, Not Fragile Plans

A rigid plan breaks under pressure.

A flexible strategy bends and adapts.

CEOs design strategies that can:

- Expand or contract
- Shift with market data
- Adjust to new opportunities
- Pivot around new threats

The goal isn't to predict the future—it's to be prepared for multiple versions of it.

Smart CEOs play both offense and defense at the same time.

---

6. Strengthen Your Emotional Discipline

When uncertainty rises, emotions rise. Fear, doubt, stress, and frustration begin to compete with logic.

The CEO mindset requires mental discipline:

- **Self-awareness** to recognize emotional triggers
- **Self-regulation** to stay calm and clear
- **Perspective** to avoid overreacting
- **Patience** to let situations unfold

A calm leader makes clearer decisions than an emotional leader.

Calm is a superpower.

---

7. Lead with Vision, Even When the Road Isn't Visible

Uncertainty can blur the next step, but it should never blur the destination.

CEOs stay anchored to their **vision**—the ultimate goal, outcome, or mission.

This vision becomes their North Star, guiding decisions even in the darkest times.

When leaders hold the vision steady, teams stay motivated and aligned.

---

8. Turn Uncertainty Into Opportunity

The greatest companies in history were built during uncertain times.

Why?

Because uncertainty unveils opportunities:

- Competitors hesitate
- Markets shift
- Customer needs evolve
- Innovation becomes necessary
- Creativity expands

A CEO looks at uncertainty and asks:

"What advantage does this moment create for us?"

This mindset turns chaos into progress.

---

9. Surround Yourself with Advisors and Data

Even the strongest CEOs don't navigate uncertainty alone.

They rely on:

- Advisors
- Analysts
- Mentors
- Industry experts

- Internal talent
- Real-time data

The goal isn't to seek permission.

The goal is to seek clarity.

Smart leaders gather insights.

Weak leaders guess.

---

10. Move Forward with Confidence

Confidence doesn't come from knowing everything.

Confidence comes from trusting yourself.

CEOs succeed in uncertainty because they:

- Trust their judgment
- Trust their preparation
- Trust their values
- Trust their team

Confidence is contagious.

When the leader stands strong, the organization stands strong.

Closing Thought for Chapter 47

Uncertainty is where leadership truly begins.

Anyone can lead when the path is clear.

It takes a CEO to lead when the path is unknown.

You don't need to eliminate uncertainty—

you simply need to develop the mindset to rise above it.

This chapter prepares you for one of the biggest responsibilities of leadership:

being the steady hand in an unsteady world.

CHAPTER 48 — The CEO Lifestyle: Habits of Elite Leaders

Being a CEO is not just a title—

it is a lifestyle, a mindset, and a daily commitment to excellence.

Elite leaders don't rise to the top by accident.

They build strong habits, protect their energy, choose discipline over comfort, and structure their lives to support high performance.

The CEO lifestyle is about being intentional with your time, your decisions, your mindset, and your actions.

It is about living in a way that elevates your leadership, sharpens your focus, and strengthens your character.

Great leaders don't hope for success—

they **live** in a way that attracts it.

---

1. CEOs Start Their Day With Intention, Not Chaos

Most people wake up reacting.

Leaders wake up preparing.

Morning habits of elite leaders include:

- Quiet time or prayer
- Planning the day
- Reviewing goals
- Clarity before movement
- Mental preparation
- Physical movement or exercise

The day is won before it begins.

---

2. They Protect Their Time Like a Valuable Asset

Time is the most valuable resource leaders have.

CEOs master time by:

- Scheduling their day
- Prioritizing high-impact tasks
- Eliminating time-wasters
- Delegating anything that doesn't require them
- Saying "no" more often

Time leadership = life leadership.

---

3. They Maintain Mental Clarity

Clarity creates confidence.

Elite leaders protect their mind by avoiding:

- Drama
- Gossip
- Negativity
- Emotional chaos
- Overthinking
- Unnecessary conflict

Their mental space stays sharp, focused, and clean.

---

4. Health Is a Leadership Priority

Energy affects leadership.

Well-being affects performance.

CEOs protect their health through:

- Regular exercise
- Nutritious eating
- Adequate sleep
- Hydration
- Stress management
- Routine health checkups

A strong body supports a strong mind.

---

5. They Read, Think, and Learn Consistently

Elite leaders feed their mind daily.

Their lifestyle includes:

- Reading books
- Studying great leaders
- Listening to audiobooks
- Learning new skills
- Staying informed
- Developing perspective

Information sharpens leadership.

---

6. CEOs Build Strong Networks and Relationships

Success grows faster with the right people.

Elite leaders:

- Build meaningful relationships
- Surround themselves with high achievers
- Seek mentors
- Connect with thinkers
- Avoid small-minded environments

Your circle fuels your growth.

---

7. They Keep Their Environment Clean and Organized

Chaos around you creates chaos inside you.

Leaders maintain:

- Clean workspaces
- Organized systems
- Structured routines
- Clutter-free environments

Organization increases productivity and reduces stress.

---

8. They Master Emotional Control

CEO lifestyle means living calmly, even when life gets loud.

They avoid:

- Anger
- Emotional breakdowns
- Impulsive decisions
- Panic reactions

Their calmness is their power.

---

9. They Prioritize Quality Over Quantity

Whether it's decisions, relationships, or tasks, CEOs choose quality.

This includes:

- High-quality conversations
- High-quality habits
- High-quality goals
- High-quality environments

Quality thinking leads to quality results.

---

10. They Create Strong Boundaries

Leaders protect their:

- Time
- Peace
- Focus
- Energy
- Commitment
- Personal standards

Boundaries make leadership sustainable.

---

11. They Make Decisions Quickly and Confidently

Indecision drains energy.

Decisiveness builds momentum.

Elite leaders:

- Analyze
- Decide
- Act
- Move forward

Confidence comes from clarity.

---

12. They Keep Their Vision Visible

The CEO lifestyle keeps the vision in front daily.

Leaders review:

- Goals
- Plans
- Strategies
- Milestones
- Desired outcomes

A visible vision creates unstoppable motivation.

---

13. They Take Care of Their Appearance

Not out of vanity—out of professionalism.

Appearance affects:

- Confidence
- Perception
- Influence
- Leadership presence

Leaders carry themselves with purpose.

---

14. They Protect Their Peace From Noise

The CEO lifestyle includes silence and reflection.

This might include:

- Meditation

- Prayer
- Sitting in quiet
- Deep thinking
- Journaling

Silence strengthens leadership clarity.

---

15. They Live With Discipline, Not Excuses

Discipline builds the lifestyle.

Excuses destroy it.

CEOs choose:

- Action over laziness
- Structure over impulse
- Growth over comfort
- Focus over distraction

Discipline is their advantage.

---

16. They End Their Day With Review and Reflection

Successful leaders close their day with intention.

They review:

- What was accomplished
- What needs improvement
- What tomorrow requires
- Lessons learned
- Opportunities gained

Reflection improves performance.

---

17. They Protect Their Personal Life and Relationships

CEO leadership doesn't ignore family, friendship, or personal happiness.

It honors them.

Strong leaders maintain:

- Healthy connections
- Time for loved ones
- Emotional awareness
- Work-life structure

Balance strengthens leadership longevity.

The CEO lifestyle is not about luxury.

It is about **leadership habits** that elevate your life, your influence, your mind, and your future.

Elite leaders live intentionally.

They think intentionally.

They act intentionally.

And because of this, everything in their life rises to a higher level.

CHAPTER 49 — Becoming the Leader People Respect and Follow

A title may give you authority—

but only character earns you **respect**.

Only consistency earns you **trust**.

And only influence earns you **followers**.

People do not follow leaders because they have to.

People follow leaders because they **want to**.

Whether you lead a team, a business, a family, or a community, your success will always come down to one truth:

You must become the kind of leader people respect, trust, and believe in.

Respect cannot be demanded.

It must be earned through daily actions, strong values, and authentic leadership.

---

1. Respect Begins With Character

People respect leaders who live with integrity.

Character includes:

- Honesty
- Accountability
- Reliability
- Consistency
- Strong moral standards

When your character is strong, people feel safe under your leadership.

---

2. Lead With Humility, Not Ego

Ego pushes people away.

Humility pulls people together.

Humble leadership means:

- Listening
- Admitting mistakes
- Respecting others
- Sharing credit
- Staying grounded

Humility builds trust faster than authority ever could.

---

3. Speak With Respect—Even When Correcting

Respectful leaders communicate with:

- Strength
- Clarity
- Professionalism
- Control

They correct without disrespect.

They lead without belittling.

They guide without attacking.

Respectful communication builds loyal followers.

---

4. Be Consistent—People Trust What They Can Predict

Nothing destroys respect faster than inconsistency.

A leader must be predictable in:

- Behavior
- Standards
- Decisions
- Reactions
- Expectations

Consistency creates stability.

Stability creates trust.

---

5. Back Your Words With Actions

People respect leaders who:

- Do what they say
- Follow through on commitments
- Honor their promises
- Keep their standards
- Lead by example

Action is the most powerful language of leadership.

---

6. Show Empathy Without Losing Authority

Empathy does not weaken leadership—

it strengthens connection.

A respected leader:

- Understands people
- Listens without judgment
- Shows compassion
- Supports growth
- Provides stability

Empathy builds loyalty.

Authority builds structure.

Great leaders balance both.

---

7. Set High Standards and Hold Everyone Accountable

People respect leaders who expect excellence.

High standards create:

- Strong teams
- Better performance
- Growth
- Discipline

- Pride in the mission

Standards show you care about the work, the people, and the vision.

---

8. Make Decisions With Fairness and Integrity

People will accept tough decisions—

if they believe they were made fairly.

Fair leaders:

- Evaluate facts
- Remove personal bias
- Stay objective
- Prioritize the mission
- Consider long-term impact

Fairness builds deep respect.

---

9. Stay Calm and Strong Under Pressure

Leaders who panic create panic.

Leaders who stay calm create confidence.

Respect grows when people see you:

- Steady
- Composed
- Secure
- Focused
- Unshaken

Calmness is leadership strength.

---

10. Treat Everyone With Dignity

Respect is built through daily interactions.

People respect leaders who treat:

- Employees
- Clients

- Staff
- Family
- Strangers

With the same level of dignity and professionalism.

Leadership is how you treat people who can do nothing for you.

---

11. Be the Example Others Want to Follow

When you carry yourself with:

- Maturity
- Confidence
- Purpose
- Honor
- Strength

People naturally follow your lead.

You become the standard, not just the supervisor.

---

12. Lead With Vision and Direction

People follow leaders who know where they're going.

Your vision gives people hope.

Your direction gives people clarity.

Your confidence gives people courage.

When your vision is strong, your leadership becomes magnetic.

---

13. Be Honest, Even When It's Hard

Honesty earns lifelong respect.

A leader must speak with:

- Truth
- Transparency
- Realness

- Courage

People trust what they can believe.

---

14. Protect the Culture—Don't Tolerate Disrespect

Respect flows downward when leadership holds the line.

Strong leaders address:

- Toxic behavior
- Disrespect
- Laziness
- Division
- Negativity

People respect leaders who protect the environment.

---

15. Make Others Better, Not Smaller

Great leaders lift people up.

They:

- Teach
- Guide
- Support
- Mentor
- Encourage
- Coach

People follow leaders who make them feel valuable and capable.

---

16. Earn Respect Through Results

Results build credibility.

People respect leaders who:

- Perform consistently
- Achieve goals
- Solve problems

- Drive progress
- Deliver outcomes

Results prove your leadership is real.

---

17. Be Authentic—Not a Performance

People follow real leaders, not actors.

Authenticity includes:

- Being genuine
- Being transparent
- Being humble
- Being human
- Being consistent

Authenticity builds trust.

Trust builds respect.

Respect builds influence.

Becoming a leader people respect and follow is not about being perfect—

it's about being committed to excellence, character, and growth.

Respect is earned through action.

Influence is built through consistency.

Leadership is measured by impact.

When you become the kind of leader people admire,

your presence inspires,

your words carry weight,

and your leadership transforms lives.

CHAPTER 50 — Stepping Into Your Next Level of Leadership

Every leader reaches a point where the next level is calling.

A point where staying the same becomes uncomfortable, and growth becomes necessary.

A point where you feel the pull to rise higher, think bigger, and lead with greater purpose.

The next level of leadership is not just about new responsibilities—

it's about becoming a stronger, wiser, more disciplined version of yourself.

Your leadership journey does not end here.

This chapter is about preparing you to step boldly into everything you are capable of becoming.

---

1. The Next Level Requires a New Version of You

The leader you were yesterday is not enough for where you're going next.

Next-level leadership requires:

- New thinking
- New habits
- New discipline
- New standards
- New decisions
- New courage

Growth requires transformation.

---

2. Upgrade Your Mindset Before You Upgrade Your Position

Mindset always comes before elevation.

To rise higher, you must think higher.

That means:

- Letting go of small thinking
- Releasing fear-based decisions
- Believing you are capable
- Seeing yourself as a leader
- Thinking with confidence and clarity

Your mindset determines your altitude.

---

3. Leave Behind What Weakens You

You cannot carry everything into your next season.

That includes:

- Limiting beliefs
- Negative environments
- Toxic people
- Old habits
- Excuses
- Fear of failure
- Fear of judgment

Growth requires subtraction as much as addition.

---

4. Build Habits That Match Your Future, Not Your Past

The habits that got you here won't get you further.

Next-level leaders adopt habits aligned with their vision:

- Daily discipline
- Continuous learning
- Clear routines
- Strategic decision-making
- Time management
- Focused action

Growth lives in your habits, not your intentions.

---

5. Strengthen Your Leadership Identity

You must see yourself as a leader before others do.

Leadership identity includes:

- Confidence
- Purpose
- Professionalism
- Emotional control
- Strong values
- Personal standards

Identity is the foundation of influence.

---

6. Invest in Your Growth Like Your Future Depends on It—Because It Does

Leaders grow intentionally.

Growth comes from:

- Books
- Courses
- Mentors
- Experience
- Reflection
- Coaching
- Mastery of skills

Your level of investment determines your level of leadership.

---

7. Get Comfortable Being Uncomfortable

Growth is uncomfortable.

Leadership is uncomfortable.

Elevation is uncomfortable.

The next level requires:

- Risk
- Courage

- Vulnerability
- Bold decisions
- Letting go of comfort zones

Comfort is the enemy of leadership.

---

8. Surround Yourself With Leaders Who Challenge You

Your environment shapes your potential.

To rise, you must connect with people who:

- Think bigger
- Expect better
- Challenge your perspective
- Hold you accountable
- Inspire growth

Your next level requires a next-level circle.

---

9. Say Yes to Opportunities That Align With Your Vision

Elevation comes through opportunity.

But not every opportunity is aligned with your destiny.

Say yes to:

- Growth
- Impact
- Leadership roles
- Skill development
- Strategic challenges

Say no to anything that distracts from your mission.

---

10. Stay Consistent When Results Are Slow

Every leader goes through seasons where:

- Progress feels invisible
- Results feel delayed
- Effort feels unnoticed

But consistency produces breakthroughs.

Stay committed even when you don't see immediate results.

That's what separates leaders from everyone else.

---

11. Master the Art of Adaptation

Your next level will demand flexibility.

Adaptation includes:

- Adjusting strategies
- Pivoting wisely
- Learning new skills
- Staying ahead of change
- Remaining open-minded

Rigid leaders break.

Adaptable leaders rise.

---

12. Lead With Purpose, Not Pressure

Pressure comes from fear of failure.

Purpose comes from commitment to impact.

When you lead with purpose:

- Stress decreases
- Clarity increases
- Confidence grows
- Leadership becomes meaningful

Purpose guides your leadership through every season.

---

13. Your Next Level Will Test You Before It Rewards You

Every elevation requires endurance.

Before the reward, you will face:

- Doubt
- Resistance

- Fear
- Challenges
- Discomfort

These are not signs of weakness—

they are signs of growth.

---

14. Celebrate How Far You've Come

Leadership is a long journey.

Take time to recognize:

- Your growth
- Your strength
- Your progress
- Your victories
- Your endurance

Reflection builds confidence for the next season.

---

15. Step Into Your Future With Strength and Certainty

Your next level is not waiting for perfection.

It is waiting for action.

You are ready for more.

You are capable of more.

You are becoming the leader your vision requires.

Your future is calling you to rise.

Step boldly.

Step confidently.

Step with purpose.

Your next level of leadership begins now.

Closing Page

Your Journey to Leadership Excellence Begins Now**

As you reach the final page of this book, remember something important: **you didn't come this far by accident.** You chose growth. You chose leadership. You chose to elevate your mindset, your habits, and your expectations.

Becoming a CEO—whether of a company, a team, or your own life—is not a title.

It is a **mindset**, a **discipline**, and a **daily commitment** to becoming your best self.

This book was never meant to simply give you information.

It was designed to ignite something within you—the drive to think bigger, act with purpose, and lead with confidence.

Now, as you step forward, carry these truths with you:

1. You Are Capable of More Than You Realize

Leadership starts with belief. Not in circumstances. Not in resources.

In yourself.

Your potential expands every time you push past fear, uncertainty, or hesitation.

You are not defined by your past—only by the standards you set moving forward.

2. The CEO Mindset Is a Daily Practice

Excellence is not created through big moments alone.

It grows through small habits, intentional actions, and the choices you make when nobody is watching.

Stay disciplined. Stay hungry. Stay consistent.

3. Growth Requires Courage

Every leader faces challenges, doubt, and discomfort.

But those who rise are those who continue anyway.

Courage is not the absence of fear—it's the refusal to let fear control your direction.

4. You Are the Leader Your Future Demands

Every chapter you've read has prepared you to elevate your standards, think strategically, and lead with strength.

Your decisions from this day forward will shape the legacy you leave behind.

5. Your Next Level Begins With the Step You Take Today

Do not close this book and return to who you were.

Move with intention.

Act with confidence.

Lead with vision.

And align every action with the successful, powerful, and disciplined version of yourself you are becoming.

Final Message

This is not the end.

It is the beginning of your next chapter as a leader.

Go forward with purpose.

Go forward with confidence.

Go forward knowing you have everything you need to build, create, and lead at a higher level.

Your mindset is your power.

Your leadership is your legacy.

Your future is waiting—step into it like a CEO.

About the Author

Cecil L. Dowdell is a leader, entrepreneur, and visionary dedicated to helping people unlock their potential and rise into the highest version of themselves. Known for his direct, powerful, and motivational approach, Cecil has spent years studying leadership, discipline, personal growth, and the mindset required to succeed at the highest levels.

Driven by a passion to inspire and uplift, Cecil turned his experiences—both victories and challenges—into a mission to guide others into stronger confidence, sharper discipline, and more influential leadership. His journey reflects resilience, courage, and an unshakable commitment to growth.

Through his work, Cecil empowers individuals to think like CEOs, lead with purpose, and build lives defined by focus, strength, and direction. His teachings continue to impact those who seek clarity, maturity, and transformation.

Cecil believes that greatness is not reserved for a chosen few—

it is available to anyone willing to develop discipline, build character, and step boldly into their purpose.

Today, Cecil continues to motivate, mentor, and lead others toward becoming the best version of themselves.

www.ingramcontent.com/pod-product-compliance
Lightning Source LLC
LaVergne TN
LVHW052300200926
848481LV00002B/426

* 9 7 9 8 2 9 5 5 2 2 5 5 0 *